The darkest places in hell are reserved for those who maintain their neutrality in times of moral crisis.

- Dante Alighieri

Human beings are a species splendid in their array of moral equipment, tragic in their propensity to misuse it, and pathetic in their constitutional ignorance of the misuse.

- Robert Wright

Why Can't You Be More Like Me?

An Introduction to Moral Philosophy

Max Malikow

Why Can't You Be More Like Me?
An Introduction to Moral Philosophy

Copyright © 2015 by Max Malikow

Published by:
Theocentric Publishing Group
1069A Main Street
Chipley, Florida 32428

www.theocentricpublishing.com

Library of Congress Control Number: 2015943582

ISBN 9780986405549

To Diane Coville, who loves unconditionally.

To Mike Lagrange, my friend who waits.

To Dr. James A. Manganello, who deserved much more and better than I gave him.

To SC, who moves me to ask: "Why can't more people be like you?"

Acknowledgments

The law of cause-and-effect posits everything owes its existence to something else. In turn, every "something else" owes its existence to an inscrutable series of prior realities. If this law is true - and I believe it is - it is impossible to produce a comprehensive list of people and events that accounts for this book. Notwithstanding, this impossibility is no excuse for not trying to give some credit where it is due.

In no predetermined order, credit is due to my publisher, Martin Murphy, who is professional, efficient, and encouraging - a rare combination indeed. I am indebted to Diane Coville, who continually yielded her rightful claim on my attention and thereby gave me time to write. As they have done before, Karen White and Terry Riley unwittingly provided delightful venues for thinking and writing. I am thankful for Rabbi Dr. Earl A. Grollman, who believed in me as a writer before I had written a single book. And I am grateful for Elie Wiesel and Nancy Kelly, who I mention together because both have exemplified sheer human decency for me.

Preface

In 1976, sitting in the audience of the Tonight Show, I saw Dr. Wayne Dyer interviewed. He was well on his way to celebrity status having written *Your Erroneous Zones*, a book that would eventually reach 35,000,000 copies sold. When one of the book's ten erroneous zones, anger, came up for discussion, Dyer suggested a question that helps him control his anger toward others: *Why can't you be more like me?* It's not a question he asks aloud, rather he thinks it to himself. It reminds him how arrogant and foolish it is to think his behavior should be the standard against which human conduct is measured.

I have forgotten much over the last thirty-eight years, but not Dr. Dyer's prescriptive question. In addition to its effectiveness for assuaging anger, it is helpful for self-regulation in interpersonal relationships. Rodney King, who attained overnight national recognition in 1991 owing to an altercation with police, asked, "Can we all get along?" (2014) Unfortunately, frequently the answer to his question is "no." Often we are indignant because someone has the audacity not to think and act more like us.

The intention of this book is to explain moral diversity and the conflict it sometimes generates between individuals, groups, and nations. Hopefully it will be helpful in our continuing effort to communicate with each other. The playwright George Bernard Shaw said, "The single biggest problem in communication is the illusion that it has taken place"

(2014). With all due respect to Shaw, I am optimistic that communication can be less an illusion and more a reality, thereby helping us to "all get along" more amicably and effectively.

Max Malikow
Syracuse, NY
July 21, 2014

Table of Contents

Introduction: What Is Moral Philosophy?

You are mistaken, my friend, if you think that a man who is worth anything ought to spend his time weighing up the prospects of life and death. He has only one thing to consider in performing any action - that is, whether he is acting rightly or wrongly, like a good man or a bad one.

- Socrates

The preface of this book provides the rationale for its title, *Why Can't You Be More Like Me?* Since prefaces go largely unread, a brief reiteration is in order. Just as one person's anger toward another can be encapsulated by the question posed by the title, so also with disagreements on matters pertaining to morality.

The August 9, 2010 cover of *Time* magazine is a disturbing portrait. It is a photograph of a disfigured, eighteen year-old Afghan girl whose nose and ears were cut off at the order of a Taliban commander. The girl, named Aisha, was sentenced to this mutilation for running away from her abusive in-laws. In a part of the world 7,000 miles from the United States the immorality in Aisha's story is not her disfigurement but fleeing from her husband's family. In that part of Afghanistan where her trial and conviction took place, her sentence was right and righteous. In other parts of the world, *Time* readers were horrified by the unconscionable, evil punishment inflicted on Aisha.

Is morality universal or particular to a given place and/or time? If morality is determined regionally then one region cannot pass judgment on another. And how can morality be universal when striking differences exist, like the one instantiated by Aisha's story? It is noteworthy that the defense used by some Nazi war criminals at the Nuremberg Trials was that they did nothing wrong. They argued the mass killing of Jewish people was neither illegal nor immoral in Nazi controlled territories.

Specific questions pursued in this book include:

- How do ethics and morals differ?

- What are the deficiencies of *absolutism* and *relativism* as moral philosophies?

- Why are humans the only moral beings?

- What are the methodologies people use for distinguishing right from wrong?

- Why is there such disparity among individuals and cultures on matters pertaining to morality?

- Is justice always moral?

- Does the end always justify the means?

- How is a moral decision to be made when duties are in conflict?

- Is morality simply a matter of having a certain feeling about something?

- Can people be good without God?

- Is a moral life always a good life and is a good life always a moral life?

Answering the question, "What is moral philosophy?" requires an understanding of philosophy in general. The word philosophy is derived from the combination of two Greek words: *philein* (love) and *sophos* (wisdom); hence philosophy's definition is "the love of wisdom." Wisdom is not to be equated with knowledge. The former is concerned with sound judgment and excellence in life management; the latter is concerned with the acquisition and understanding of facts. A person can be knowledgeable without being wise. Biblical scholar Luke Timothy Johnson expressed this when he wrote:

> Classical Greek philosophers Socrates, Aristotle, and Plato are fine - if thinking is what you want. But the word philosophy means "love of wisdom," not "love of thinking." What about solid advice about how to be a good father or friend; or how to grow old gracefully; or know what true happiness is? Where can you find philosophy that tells you not how to think well, but how to live well" (2007, p. 40)?

The renowned nineteenth century philosopher and psychologist William James voiced the same thought in fewer words: "The philosophy which is so important in each of us is not a technical matter; it is more or less a silent sense of what life honestly and deeply means" (1995, p. 1).

As a scholarly pursuit, philosophy consists of six subcategories, each of which corresponds to a question:

- epistemology: How can we be certain about anything we claim to be true?

- logic: How can we be certain that a conclusion is the result of a reliable reasoning process?

- ethics: Are there standards and methodologies for determining morality?

- value theory: What are the factors that give one thing more worth than another?

- aesthetics: What makes something pleasing or displeasing to the senses?

- metaphysics: Is there reality outside of the material realm that cannot be perceived by the senses or subjected to scientific investigation?

Are ethics and morals synonymous?

Colloquially, *ethics* and *morals* are used interchangeably. Certainly they are similar in that both relate to "right" and "wrong" conduct. Technically, there is a distinction between the two: ethics refers to a set of rules provided to an individual by an external source; *morals* refer to an individual's self-determined principles regarding proper conduct. Many professions have *ethical* guidelines; for example, physicians pledge to uphold the Hippocratic Oath. The individual who believes "honesty is the best policy" and lives accordingly has made a personal *moral* commitment. This distinction notwithstanding, in the pages that follow *ethics* and *morals* will be used interchangeably unless otherwise stated.

What is ethics?

As stated above, ethics is one of six subcategories of philosophy. Further, since decisions about "right" and "wrong" often involve the relative worth of things, pain and pleasure, and the possibility of a supreme being, ethics is related to the subcategories of value theory, aesthetics, and metaphysics.

What is ethical deliberation?

Contemplating the rightness or wrongness of an action requires considering four questions:

1. What are the relevant facts?

2. What are the accepted principles for this situation?

3. What is the proper application of these principles to this situation?

4. What is the action that should (or should not) be taken?

Two examples from history that might be helpful in understanding ethical deliberation are separate situations; one involved a medical doctor and the other a clergyman. In September of 1939 Sigmund Freud, 83 years-old and suffering with cancer, asked his physician, Max Schur, to administer a lethal dose of morphine. Dr. Schur complied, thereby violating the Hippocratic Oath's prohibition against giving a deadly medication to a patient. However, that same oath requires physicians to exercise sound judgment and act in the best interest of their patients. In this case, Dr. Schur determined it was in Freud's best interest to bring his suffering to an end. (Noteworthy is Freud was a physician and could have self-injected the morphine. Was it ethical for Freud to orchestrate this dilemma for Dr. Schur?)

In his "Letter from Birmingham Jail" the Rev. Dr. Martin Luther King, Jr. asserted all people have a moral responsibility to disobey unjust laws. He was in jail for disobeying a court order that prohibited mass parades and demonstrations without a proper permit. Judge W.A. Jenkins had ruled such demonstrations disturb the peace. In his letter, Dr. King asserted citizens bear simultaneous responsibilities to obey just laws and disobey those that are unjust. His letter provided a criterion for discerning inequitable laws:

> One may well ask, "How can you advocate breaking some laws and obeying others?" The answer is found in the fact that there are two types of laws: there are just laws, and there are unjust laws. I would agree with St. Augustine that "An unjust law is no law at all." Now, what is the difference between the two? How does one determine when a law is just or unjust? A just law is a man-made code that squares with the moral law, or the law of God. An unjust law is a code that is out of harmony with the moral law. To put it in the terms of St. Thomas Aquinas, an unjust law is a human law that is not rooted in eternal and natural law. Any law that uplifts human personality is just. Any law that degrades human personality is unjust (04/16/1963).

The actions of these two men illustrate the four issues constituting ethical deliberation. For Dr. Schur, the *relevant facts* were Freud's suffering and request for relief. For Rev. King they were institutionalized because of racial segregation and the perpetuation of an unjust law in Birmingham, Alabama. Concerning the *accepted principles*, Schur had to wrestle with the Hippocratic Oath and King had to weigh law-abiding citizenship against compliance with an unjust law. In their respective *situations*, both men determined one principle would have to yield to another. Concerning *action*, Schur engaged in physician-assisted suicide and King opted for civil disobedience.

What is ethical theory?

The work of ethical theory is to evaluate and establish principles by which moral problems might be solved. Again, an event from history provides an explanatory illustration. Arguably the most significant decision in the history of warfare is President Harry S. Truman's resolution to drop atomic bombs on the Japanese cities of Hiroshima and Nagasaki. This momentous decision is consistent with the sign on his desk with the inscription, "The buck stops here," as well as his oft quoted, "If you can't stand the heat, get out of the kitchen" (2014).

Is it possible to justify the intentional killing of an estimated 100,000 civilians and injuring of an equal number? President Truman applied the ethical principle of *utilitarianism* in defending his decision. *Utilitarianism* is the ethical theory that posits morally right actions are those that result in the greatest good for the most number of involved people. He reasoned the alternative to deployment of atomic bombs would have been a land invasion of the Japanese islands, resulting in many more dead and wounded. Of course, most of the dead and wounded would have been military personnel. Acknowledging this, he maintained his responsibility as President of the United States was to minimize American casualties and end the war in America's favor as soon as possible.

Another example from the same era is an account from the Holocaust in which a woman named Sophie suffocated her infant to prevent discovery by the Gestapo. In hiding with approximately fifteen other Jews, the crying infant would have divulged their location and resulted in their removal to a concentration camp and death for some if not all of them (Matousek, 2011, p. 112). A utilitarian evaluation of this story would conclude that suffocating the baby was the right moral action.

In both cases, the "greatest good" principle propounded by *utilitarianism* provides a guideline for the moral evaluation of the actions of President Truman and the Jewish woman.

Why study ethics?

As a subcategory of philosophy, the study of ethics has the potential to help us live better. (Recall Professor Johnson's assertion that the purpose of philosophy is not to enable us to think better, but to live better.) Another benefit of studying ethics is its potential for improving interpersonal skill. Engaging in an effort to understand moral beliefs with which we disagree enhances our ability to understand other people.

Introduction: What is Moral Philosophy

How are morality, immorality, and amorality different?

A dictionary definition of *morality* is, "beliefs about what is right behavior and what is wrong behavior" (1973). It is derived from the Latin *moralitas*, which means, "manner, character, proper behavior."

Although *immorality* is often understood as evil or wickedness, it can also mean *behavior that is contrary to a culture's established principles of right conduct*. This latter understanding suggests a culture's established principles might be evil and the individual who rebels against them would be acting honorably. Anti-Nazi theologians Martin Niemoller and Dietrich Bonhoeffer embodied such rebellion and were imprisoned for it. Eventually, Bonhoeffer was executed as a traitor. The abolitionist John Brown believed only an armed insurrection would bring about an end to slavery at a time when it was widely accepted in the United States. Like Bonhoeffer, he was convicted of treason and hanged. Yet, today a monument stands to John Brown in Harper's Ferry, West Virginia where the insurrection took place. Such defiance of authority and convention is what the existentialist philosopher Albert Camus had in mind when he wrote: "The only way to deal with an un-free world is to become so absolutely free that your very existence is an act of rebellion" (Malikow, 2014, p. 25).

Amorality is indifference toward the principles of right conduct. The serial murderer Richard Kuklinski, also known as "The Iceman," claimed to have killed over 250 people, the first when he was 13 years-old. His self-description, "I am what I am, and the truth is I don't give a flying (expletive deleted) what anyone

9

thinks of me," characterizes him as the epitome of amorality (Malikow, 2013, p. 41).

I. What Makes an Issue a Moral Issue?

Art, like morality, consists in drawing a line somewhere.
                                                    - G.K. Chesterson

One method for distinguishing moral issues from issues of other types (e.g. economic, legal or medical) is an inductive approach. Reasoning inductively means using a specific example to reach a general conclusion. Consider capital punishment, also referred to as the death penalty. In the United States thirty-two states allow for capital punishment, eighteen do not. Undisputedly, capital punishment is a legal issue; but it is no less a moral issue. As such, it is a specific example useful for inductively establishing criteria for determining what constitutes a moral issue. The remainder of this chapter describes six criteria with no claim that they are the only six.

1. A moral issue involves the rightness or wrongness of an action.

Capital punishment arouses a spirited debate concerning the rectitude of putting a person to death as the penalty for a crime. While there is controversy about the most humane method for execution and disagreement concerning its effectiveness as a crime deterrent, neither addresses the "rightness" of state sanctioned killing. The argument that an innocent person might erroneously be executed is a practical argument against the death penalty. The argument that an executed murderer will never again kill is a pragmatic argument in favor of the death penalty. Neither of these assertions contributes to a moral argument on either side of the issue.

2. *A moral issue involves at least one widely accepted ethical principle.*

Opponents of capital punishment assert the sacredness of life as a moral injunction against capital punishment. Ironically, Senator Orrin Hatch (Republican, Utah) expressed support for the death penalty citing the same principle: "Capital punishment is our society's recognition of the sanctity of life" (2014). Regarding the sanctity of life, both sides of this debate have been known to quote from the Bible. This is possible because the same Bible that commands, "Thou shalt not kill," (Exodus 20:13) also prescribes the death penalty for murder (Exodus 21:12-14; Leviticus 24:17, 21) and adultery (Leviticus 20:10; Deuteronomy 22:22-24). Either the Bible contains a stunning contradiction or it implies not all killing is unlawful murder.

Opponents of the death penalty also cite the Eighth Amendment of the *United States Constitution's* prohibition of "cruel and unusual punishment." They argue that an execution inflicts unacceptable pain, suffering, and humiliation. This makes it "cruel and unusual" and, therefore, unconstitutional. In *Furman v. Georgia* (1972), Justice William Brennan included a definition of "cruel and unusual punishment" in his decision: "A severe punishment that is clearly and totally rejected by society." Proponents of the death penalty disagree with Brennan, arguing even if they do not represent society's majority view, the reality of the debate proves capital punishment is not "clearly and totally rejected" by society.

3. *A moral issue involves a decision affecting at least one person other than the decision-maker.*

Anyone directly or indirectly associated with an execution is affected by it. The convicted who is put to death is the most obvious person. However, to lesser and varying degrees, juries, witnesses, judges, and prosecuting attorneys are affected by a state legislature's decision to include capital punishment in their state's penal code. Participating in any way in the killing of another person leaves an impression on virtually anyone who is not a sociopath.

4. *A moral issue involves the assumption of responsibility.*

In his speech at the 1968 Republican National Convention, then California Governor Ronald Reagan advocated capital punishment citing a moral argument: "We must reject the idea that every time a law's broken, society is guilty rather than the lawbreaker. It is time to restore the American precept that each individual is accountable for his actions" (07/31/1968). Psychiatrist M. Scott Peck expressed agreement with Mr. Reagan with this thought from *The People of the Lie:*

Triggers are pulled by individuals. Orders are given and executed by individuals. In the last analysis, every single human act is ultimately the result of an individual choice

(1983, p. 215).

Just as the convicted is the one most obviously affected by his execution, he is also the one most responsible for it. (Assuming, of course, he was rightfully convicted.) And, just as juries, witnesses, judges, and prosecuting attorneys are affected by their participation in an execution, they also are responsible for their part in it. State legislators who voted in favor of the death penalty and medical personnel who participate in an execution also are responsible for their contributions to an execution. In his analysis of the Holocaust, Rabbi Richard Rubenstein explained its implementation and accomplishment in terms of a sophisticated division of labor resulting in a dispersion of responsibility (1975). Nevertheless, even when responsibility for an act can be distributed widely, each contributor bears her share of responsibility.

5. A moral issue involves at least one of the "seven deadly sins."

Introduced by Pope Gregory (540-604 A.D.) and repeated in Dante Alighieri's 14th century epic poem, "The Divine Comedy," the seven deadly sins are pride, envy, anger, sloth (laziness), avarice (greed), gluttony, and lust. When the death penalty is invoked, anger is expressed by many, who are aware of the crime, especially those touched personally by the criminal act. Coincidentally, anger might have been the driving force for the crime. This is not to say all capital offenses are motivated by anger. Lust, the strong desire for sexual gratification, greed, and envy are all capable of motivating the worst of criminal acts.

If pride is understood as pleasure derived from a sense of achievement, opponents of capital punishment could argue the deadly sin of pride is a part of executions. They would contend proponents of the death penalty derive satisfaction from executions from the illusion that justice has been accomplished.

6. A moral issue involves at least one of the four cardinal virtues.

The four cardinal virtues are fortitude (courage), temperance (self-control), justice (fairness), and prudence (wisdom). They are referred to in Plato's *Republic* (Book IV, 426-435) and were introduced into theological literature in the 4th century A.D. by St. Ambrose and St. Augustine. A moral issue involves at least one of these virtues. It is undisputed that some crimes are so heinous they challenge the self-restraint of those entrusted with fulfilling justice by punishing the offender. Opponents of capital punishment insist the impulse to impose the death penalty must be subdued in such cases. In addition, they would argue the strong and unreflective urge to act must yield to wisdom, in instances of "not guilty by reason of mental defect." Prudence is required to determine if diminished capacity of those accused exempt them from responsibility for the crime.

Conclusion

On May 21, 1924 two wealthy University of Chicago law students, Nathan Leopold and Richard Loeb, abducted 14-year-old Bobby Frank, bludgeoned him with a chisel, and stuffed his body in a culvert. It was presented at trial that Leopold and Loeb were enthralled by Friedrich Nietzsche's idea that society's concepts of good and evil do not apply to those who have the temerity to rise above social expectations. It was not so much the idea of murder that attracted Leopold and Loeb, but the idea of getting away with murder as a demonstration of their superior intellect and boldness.

Their defense attorney, Clarence Darrow, entered a plea of guilty in order to proceed to the sentencing phase and argue before the judge rather than the jury. Darrow was hopeful of convincing the judge to sentences of life imprisonment rather than executions. His singular, eloquent argument included,

> Is any blame attached because somebody took Nietzsche's philosophy seriously and fashioned a life upon it? ... it is hardly fair to hang a 19 year-old boy for the philosophy that was taught him at a university (Darrow, 08/22/24).

Pointing to their ages and the influence of their education, Darrow appealed to Judge John R. Caverly to consider Leopold and Loeb not fully responsible for their abhorrent crime. His twelve-hour plea convinced the judge that death sentences would not constitute justice. Richard Loeb died in prison in 1936, murdered by a fellow inmate. Nathan Leopold, was paroled in 1958 and died of a heart attack in 1971.

II. Why Are Humans the Only Moral Beings?

A man without ethics is a wild beast loosed upon the world.
                                                    - Albert Camus

You have brains in your head. You have feet in your shoes.
You can steer yourself in any direction you choose.
                                    - Dr. Seuss (Theodore Geisel)

The playwright Pierre-Augusten Caron Beaumarchais wrote, "Drinking when we are not thirsty and making love all year round, madam, that is all there is to distinguish us from other animals" (Malikow, 2013, p. 161). In *Why Zebras Don't Get Ulcers*, neuroscientist Robert Sapolsky explains it is the unique ability of human beings to imagine the future that generates anxiety and accounts for why we get ulcers and animals do not (1994). Beaumarchais' proposal is limited; there is more than untimely drinking and seasonally unrestricted love-making that distinguishes us from other animals. Sapolsky's assertion also is limited in that it is not merely envisioning the future that generates human anxiety. The burden of free will and the responsibility that accompanies it also create anxiety. In fact, worrying about the future and ruminating over decision-making were sufficient for Soren Kierkegaard to characterize anxiety as "the natural state of human beings" (Menand, 2014).

Making choices, imagining consequences, and being responsible make human beings unique in the pantheon of living things as the only moral beings. As Mark Twain wryly observed, "Man is the only animal that blushes. Or needs to" (Negri, 1999, p. 1).

In *Consider the Lobster: And Other Essays* David Foster Wallace invites the reader to consider whether lobsters experience pain when submerged in boiling water (2007). He suggests they might, thereby insinuating eating lobster is a moral issue. In 2007 professional football player Michael Vick was sentenced to twenty-one months in prison for his inhumane treatment of dogs as part of a dogfighting competition. The International Union for Conservation of Nature has designated over 3,000 animals as an "endangered species," meaning they are vulnerable to extinction unless human beings cooperate in protective measures. Consider the following narrative from the ethics section of an introductory philosophy textbook:

Winchester, Massachusetts is a quaint little town located seven miles north of Boston. Its numerous colonial homes fronted by impeccably manicured lawns and charming town center contribute to Winchester being one of New England's priciest communities. Not that any town would have disregarded the invasion, but the pristine state of Winchester prior to the arrival of the geese made their intrusion especially troubling.

These were Canada geese, a breed so large that they walked about fearlessly with an air of entitlement. A child licking an ice cream cone or snacking on a cookie in proximity to the geese did so at risk. Hundreds of these geese deployed as dozens of flocks deposited their cigar-sized droppings all over town, as if to mark their territory. When the undeniable became intolerable, a town meeting was called to address the problem. Subsequent meetings became necessary as each attempt to relocate the unwanted birds failed.

Eventually, there came the meeting at which killing the geese was discussed. Those who advocated termination suggested paying hunters a bounty for each goose carcass. Some at the meeting rejected this strategy, citing an understandable safety concern. Still others at the meeting made an impassioned moral plea against killing the intruders on the ground that the birds had a right to live, however bothersome and repugnant they might be (Malikow, 2009, p. 13).

Those who argued the geese had an inviolable right to live believed the citizens of Winchester had an obligation to accommodate to the geese. Because of their size, Canada geese have few natural predators. However, they are a food source for coyotes, wolves, falcons, owls, and eagles; none of which have a moral obligation to restrain from killing the geese. Only humans have town meetings to discuss killing geese.

Animal and Human Survival Instinct

An evolutionary approach to psychology includes the assertion there are two fundamental human drives: survival and reproduction. If this is correct, human beings are no different from all other species. However, unlike all other organisms, human beings are capable of overriding the survival instinct and committing suicide. Even when some animals and insects seem to have committed suicide, they have not done so. Insect and animal self-sacrificial deaths are not suicides because they do not involve deliberation. These deaths are not self-determined but an innate reaction to a certain set of conditions. (Thomas Joiner has elaborated on this phenomenon at length in his book, *Myths About Suicide*, Harvard University Press, 2011.) Some aphids will explode when a wasp has deposited its eggs inside the aphid for their incubation. Similarly, Malaysian ants will explode as an ultimate act of defense against nest invaders.

Self-detonating aphids and ants are fascinating as entomological occurrences, but neither is a moral issue. On the other hand, self-determined deaths by human beings are suitable for ethical discussions. The French sociologist Emile Durkheim classified suicide into four categories, one of which he designated *altruistic suicide* (1897). Self-sacrifice is the defining feature of this type of suicide. An altruistic suicide is a self-determined death motivated by what is perceived as a service to another person or persons. In her bestselling memoir, *An Unquiet Mind*, psychologist Kay Jamison provides a moving description of an altruistic suicide, recalled from her childhood when she and her classmates were on recess in a playground.

> I was standing with my head back, one pigtail caught between my teeth, listening to the jet overhead. The noise was loud, unusually so, which meant that it was close. My elementary school was near Andrews Air Force Base, just outside of Washington; many of us were

pilots' kids, so the sound was a matter of routine. ... The noise of the jet became louder, and I saw the other children in my second-grade class dart their heads upward. The plane was coming in very low, then it streaked past us, scarcely missing the playground. As we stood there clumped together, it flew into the trees, exploding directly in front of us. ... Over the next few days it became clear from the release of the young pilot's final message to the control tower before he died, that he knew he could save his own life by bailing out. He also knew, however, that by doing so he risked that his unaccompanied plane would fall onto the playground and kill those of us who were there.

The dead pilot became a hero, transformed into a scorchingly vivid, completely impossible ideal for what was meant by the concept of duty. ... The memory of the crash came back to me many times over the years, as a reminder both of how one aspires after and needs such ideals, and how killingly difficult it is to achieve them. I never again looked at the sky and saw only vastness and beauty. From that afternoon on I saw that death was also and always there (1995, pp. 11-13).

When a pain-riddled, fully cognizant patient has requested a lethal injection, as occurred in 1998 when Thomas Youk appealed to Dr. Jack Kevorkian to administer one, a *rational suicide* has occurred. (Durkheim referred to these as *fatalistic suicides*.) Youk, age 52, was in the final stages of amyotrophic lateral sclerosis (a.k.a. Lou Gehrig's disease). Be it altruistic or rational, only a human being can engage in a premeditated, intentional, self-enacted death. This is not the case with the aphids, ants (or lemmels or redback spiders or bumble bees). Even when soldiers obediently follow orders that take them to their death, they are acting from their training, not instinct. This is what makes Tennyson's "six hundred" heroic in "The Charge of the Light Brigade." When he wrote of them, "Theirs not to reason why, Theirs but to do and die," it was in recognition of their bravery, not a description of their obtuseness (1854).

Conscience and the Psychopath

When Shakespeare wrote, "Conscience doth make cowards of us all" he was referring to the feeling within that restrains dubious behavior (*Hamlet*, Act III, scene 1). But what of those who know no such restraint? Dr. Robert Hare, who conducted research on psychopaths for over twenty-five years, offers this definition:

> (A psychopath) is a self-centered, callous, and remorseless person profoundly lacking in empathy and the ability to form warm emotional relationships with others, a person who functions without the restraints of conscience. (They) are lacking the very qualities that allow human beings to live in social harmony (1999, p. 2).

The aforementioned serial murderer, Richard Kuklinski (Introduction), who claimed indifference to what anyone might think of him is an avatar of Dr. Hare's definition. A person lacking a conscience or whose conscience is blunted by disease or injury is a seriously impaired human being. The word unconscionable literally means to be unguided by conscience. Only human beings can act *unconscionably* because only human beings have a conscience.

Free Will vs. Determinism

Simply stated, *free will* is the ability to engage in authentic choice-making. While decision making is always influenced by relevant factors, influences are not irresistible forces. Aristotle advocated for free will when he asserted, "What it lies in our power to do, it lies also in our power not to do" (2014). Other advocates for free will posit without free will it would be impossible to hold people responsible for their behavior. Moreover, the philosopher Thomas Ellis Katen believes free will is a defining feature of human beings:

> Which makes most sense of and best illustrates the facts of human experience as we know them? If the issue is put in these terms, I think the position could be developed that the idea of freedom is an inherent part of the defining concept of man (1973, p. 318).

In contrast to free will, *determinism* is the belief that human actions are not chosen but compelled by circumstances and conditioning. Supporting determinism is the *law of cause-and-effect* which assumes nothing is the cause of itself. In other words, everything that exists owes its existence to something prior to itself. (The only exception would be something that is eternal, if there is such a thing. This is a metaphysical issue.) The French philosopher Paul Holbach believed, "every event is the necessary outcome of a cause or set of causes" (p. 313). He wrote:

> Man's life is a line that nature commands him to describe upon the earth, without his ever being able to swerve from it ... even for an instant. ... Nevertheless, in spite of the shackles by which he is bound, it is pretended that he is a free agent (1770, p. 1).

The centuries old *free will* vs. *determinism debate* is relevant to moral philosophy because without free will there can be no moral decision-making. Without free will, every human action would be compelled by prior causes. This would mean just as insects and animals operate on instinct and bear no responsibility for anything they do, human beings would not be responsible for their actions since choice is an illusion.

Paraphrasing the 19th century German philosopher, Arthur Schopenhauer, *a man can do what he desires, but he cannot choose what to desire.* This thought allows for both authentic decision-making (free will) and the law of cause-and-effect (determinism). While we are not responsible for every thought and desire that occurs to us, we are responsible for managing them once they occur. Causation is not coercion; we are not as animals and insects acting on instinct.

Under what conditions are people not responsible for their behavior?

II. Why Are Humans the Only Moral Beings?

On September 18, 1848 a Rutland and Burlington Rail road foreman named Phineas Gage had what is perhaps history's best-known industrial accident. An explosion drove a 3'7" iron rod through his head, entering under his left eye and exiting out of the top of his skull. Amazingly, Gage survived the ordeal, although he lost his left eye and suffered a partial facial paralysis. However, the most serious injury was to his brain. The passage of the rod severely damaged his left frontal cortex, the part of the brain responsible for impulse control. Until his death, a dozen years later, Gage's behavior was unrestrained, given to fits of uncontrollable rage and rantings. It does not require an education in neurology to understand why Phineas Gage was not responsible for his volatile behavior.

In addition to appreciating how a brain injury can affect behavior, it is informative to entertain the question of when people are not legally responsible for their conduct. In jurisprudence the standard for *not guilty by reason of mental defect* is the M'Naghten Rule. According to this rule an accused is not responsible for a criminal act if he is incapable of distinguishing "right" from "wrong" conduct or incapable of behaving in conformity to the law, even if he understands "right" and "wrong." An example of someone incapable of distinguishing "right" from "wrong" is Peter Carlquist, a psychiatric patient with paranoid schizophrenia. Several years ago, in full public view, he stabbed nine year-old Katie Mason to death (Nuland, 1993, p. 124). An example of someone incapable of conforming her behavior to the law in spite of a knowledge of "right" and "wrong" is Andrea Yates. In 2001 she drowned her five children, ranging in age from seven years to six months, in a bathtub and then called the police. Her diagnosis was postpartum depression and postpartum psychosis. Found not guilty by reason of mental defect, she remains imprisoned in a psychiatric facility.

A third legal category by which an individual is not responsible for a crime is acting on an *irresistible impulse*. Commonly referred to as "crimes of passion" and "temporary insanity," an *irresistible impulse* arises under extraordinary conditions. An example from fiction is John Grisham's novel, *A Time to Kill* (1989), in which a father murders the two men who raped and maimed his ten year-old daughter.

III. How Do People Determine Right from Wrong?

Always behave in such a way that you'll never be ashamed of the truth about yourself.

- Fred "Mister" Rogers

If you obsess over whether you are making the right decision, you are basically assuming that the universe will reward you for one thing and punish you for another. The universe has no fixed agenda. Once you make any decision, it works around that decision.

Deepak Chopra

The following moral dilemma, created by psychologist Jonathan Haidt, provides an opportunity to consider the basis upon which certain behaviors are considered immoral.

Julie and Mark are brother and sister. They are traveling together in France on summer vacation from college. One night they are staying alone together in a cabin near the beach. They decide it would be very interesting and fun if they tried making love. At the very least, it would be a new experience for each of them. Julie was already taking birth control pills, but Mark uses a condom too, just to be safe. They both enjoy making love, but they decide to never do it again. They keep that night as a special secret, which makes them feel even closer to each other. What do you think about that? Was it o.k. for them to make love? (2006, pp. 20-21)

If you believe Julie and Mark acted immorally, on what did you base your judgment? It cannot be on practical grounds, since neither a sexually transmitted disease nor a pregnancy was a possibility. It might be on legal grounds, but the laws against incest vary from country to country and from state to state within the United States. Moreover, a conviction would require a confession by either Mark or Julie and probably both of them.

If you consider their sexual experiment immoral, this would raise the question, "Whose morality?" The Hebrew Bible forbids various forms of incest (Leviticus 18:8-18; 20:11-21) and the New Testament denounces a case of adultery in one of the Pauline epistles (1Corinthians 5:1-5). If the biblical prohibition of incest is understood as God's way of preventing birth defects then the religious prohibition is actually rooted in a practical consideration. This would mean if no pregnancy could occur, as with Julie and Mark, then arguably there is nothing wrong with their lovemaking.

Over centuries, philosophers, theologians, and psychologists have offered diverse suggestions for distinguishing "right" from "wrong" conduct. The balance of this chapter addresses eight of these proposals.

Divine Inspiration

The tombstone inscription of the eighteenth century German philosopher Immanuel Kant reads: "Two things fill my mind with ever increasing awe, the starry heavens above me and the moral law within me" (1785). He believed the Creator of the universe is also responsible for the moral compass within each human being. Kant marveled that his moral conduct was of interest to the architect of the cosmos and elaborated on this thought by describing a metaphorical wall separating the subjective reality (*phenomena*) from objective reality (*noumena*). He believed humankind exists in the subjective, physical realm and has no access to the objective, nonphysical domain, inhabited by God. However, Kant noted one exception, that being the conscience, provided by God so human beings could conduct themselves with a sense of how they ought to live. He also distinguished criminal conduct from conscience when he wrote: "In law a man is guilty when he violates the rights of others. In ethics he is guilty if he only thinks of doing so" (2014).

Kant further believed since moral precepts derive from God, they are to be followed without exception, making them absolute. Kant's approach to ethics is *deontological*, derived from the Greek word *deon*, which means duty. The idea that right and wrong vary from person to person, situation to situation, culture to culture or time to time was an abomination to Kant. In his *Grounding for the Metaphysics of Morals* (1785) he used the term *categorical imperatives* in reference to principles of conduct that are to be followed regardless of circumstances. Three of these imperatives are *universalization, human dignity*, and *reciprocity*. *Universalization* guides moral conduct by asking: Would the world be a better place if everyone acted as you are about to act? *Human dignity* asserts people are never to be employed as a means to an end because nothing is more important than a human being. *Reciprocity* asks: If you were a king who could decree laws by which others would have to live, would you be willing to live under the laws you would decree?

Sentimentalism

In common parlance *sentimental* refers to someone who is excessively prone to feelings of tenderness, sadness or nostalgia. This understanding also applies to *sentimentalism* in moral philosophy, meaning right and wrong exist as feelings rather than concepts. The well-known conundrum of whether there is noise when a tree falls in an unpopulated forest is parallel to whether *right* and *wrong* exist as entities apart from human experience. Sentimentalists like David Hume maintain right and wrong do not exist until someone has a feeling about an event or circumstance.

A fascinating experiment conducted by British psychologist Bruce Hood provides a striking example of the human proclivity to make choices based on sentiment rather than reason. In his investigation, he offered people 10 pounds (approximately $15) if they would wear the sweater he held before them. Nearly everyone agreed until they were told the cardigan once belonged to Fred West, a notorious serial murderer who had abducted and killed a dozen women. After learning of the sweater's previous owner, almost everyone who had agreed to wear the sweater then refused to do so. When asked why they had changed their mind, none of the participants could offer a rational explanation. Instead, in various ways, they said, "It just wouldn't *feel* right to have that on my body." Such an explanation brings to mind Blaise Pascal's assertion: "The heart has its reasons of which reason knows nothing" (2014). In *A Treatise of Human Nature* (1740) Hume characterized reason as enslaved to passion and completely impotent in moral decision-making, serving only an advisory role in moral deliberations. It's difficult to disagree with him given the frequency with which people admit to having acted contrarily to reason. A well-publicized survival story supports Hume's assertion that passion trumps other factors when contemplating a moral act. In 1972 a plane carrying a Uruguayan rugby team crashed in the Andes Mountains, killing twenty-nine of the forty-five passengers. Some of the sixteen survivors resorted to cannibalism in order to stay alive. They *felt* survival justified eating from the bodies of the deceased. Those who refused to eat from the dead *felt* doing so would be morally wrong.

Utilitarianism

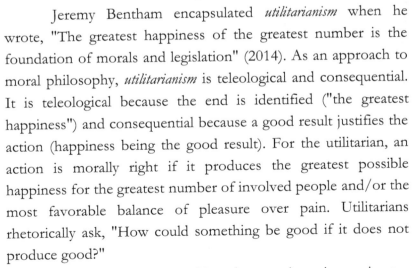

Jeremy Bentham encapsulated *utilitarianism* when he wrote, "The greatest happiness of the greatest number is the foundation of morals and legislation" (2014). As an approach to moral philosophy, *utilitarianism* is teleological and consequential. It is teleological because the end is identified ("the greatest happiness") and consequential because a good result justifies the action (happiness being the good result). For the utilitarian, an action is morally right if it produces the greatest possible happiness for the greatest number of involved people and/or the most favorable balance of pleasure over pain. Utilitarians rhetorically ask, "How could something be good if it does not produce good?"

Utilitarianism has appeal in a democratic society owing to its deference to the majority. Further, it stresses impartiality in that everyone's happiness counts the same. Another utilitarian, John Stuart Mill, addressed the good of the majority and impartiality with these words: "The only freedom which deserves the name is that of pursuing our own good, in our own way, so long as we do not attempt to deprive others of theirs, or impede their efforts to obtain it" (2014).

Utilitarianism is not without its critics. David Hume questioned it on the ground that neither the "greatest good" nor the "greatest number" could be calibrated. A consideration of the atomic bombings of Hiroshima and Nagasaki in World War II elucidates Hume's argument against *utilitarianism*. President Harry S. Truman defended his decision to use the ultimate weapon of that time with this statement:

> Having found the bomb we have used it. We have used it against those who attacked us without warning at Pearl Harbor, against those who have starved and beaten and executed American prisoners of war, against those who have abandoned all pretense of obeying international laws of warfare. We have used it in order to shorten the agony of war, in order to save the lives of thousands and thousands of young Americans. We will continue to use it until we completely destroy Japan's power to make war. Only a Japanese surrender will stop us. ... When you have to deal with a beast, you have to treat him as a beast. It is most regrettable but nevertheless true (08/06/1945).

Teleologically, the President's argument is irrefutable if the consequences are limited to the "greatest good" of the United States. However, his decision is vulnerable to criticism if "greatest good" is expanded to include the estimated 150,000 Japanese civilians killed in the two bombings. Moreover, the well-known axiom, "All is fair in love and war," notwithstanding, the 1949 Geneva Convention reaffirmed and formalized the understanding that lethal action against noncombatants is unethical.

Situational Ethics/Relativism

The name Joseph Fletcher is virtually synonymous with *situational ethics*, largely due to his controversial book, *Situational Ethics: The New Morality* (1966). An ordained Episcopal minister and seminary professor, he eventually declared himself an atheist. Nevertheless, he agreed with the biblical precept, "Love thy neighbour" (Mark 12:31) and wrote: "Love wills the neighbor's good, whether we like him or not" (1966, p. 120).

Situational ethics is a relativistic approach to morality because it asserts there are no moral absolutes. Hence, an action that is morally wrong in one situation can be morally right in another. For Fletcher, the guiding principle for moral conduct is *agape*, the Greek word for "unselfish, outgoing affection or tenderness for another without necessarily expecting anything in return" (Hill, 1987, p. 538). Among his controversial views were the moral rectitude of abortions, euthanasia, and suicide if they are motivated by love.

He argued absolute, abstract laws of morality are meaningless and must give way to the most loving action in a given situation. In fact, Fletcher saw love as the defining characteristic of morality: "We ought to love people and use things; the essence of immorality is to love things and use people" (2014). Accordingly, he believed an action acquires the status of rectitude when it is the most loving thing to do.

A striking illustration of situational ethics is found in John Steinbeck's classic novel *Of Mice and Men*. Under normal circumstances the thought of fatally shooting an unarmed man is reprehensible. However, the story ends with George shooting Lenny, a mentally retarded gentle giant. Literally not knowing his own strength, Lenny unintentionally kills a woman. Rather than have Lenny face the cruelty of the posse closing in on him and either life imprisonment or execution, George shoots Lenny as an act of compassion.

Obedience to Authority

Quoted in chapter one are these words of the renowned psychiatrist and author M. Scott Peck: "Triggers are pulled by individuals. Orders are given and executed by individuals. In the last analysis, every single human act is ultimately the result of an individual choice" (1983, p. 215). This being said, what are the possibilities when individuals believe they are *not* responsible for their actions? One of best-known experiments in psychological history provides an answer. In 1961 Stanley Milgram conducted an experiment to determine the extent to which people will follow an order given by an authority figure. In the experiment subjects were ordered to administer painful electric shocks to other subjects. (The shocks were *not* real. The receiving subjects *acted* as though they were being shocked and the administering subjects believed the shocks to be real.)

The pseudo-shocks graduated from 15 to 450 volts in 15 volt increments. Milgram and the psychological professionals he consulted before the experiment predicted less than one-percent of the subjects administering the shocks would obey the order of the authority figure (the supervising psychologist) to continue shocking up to 450 volts. The only actual shock in the experiment was the one experienced by Milgram. Sixty-five percent of the administering subjects continued shocking up to the maximum voltage.

In an article written thirteen years after his study, Milgram reflected:

Ordinary people, simply doing their jobs, and without any particular hostility on their part, can become agents in a terrible destructive process. Moreover, even when the destructive effects of their work become patently clear, and they are asked to carry out actions incompatible with fundamental standards of morality, relatively few people have the resources needed to resist authority (1974).

One explanation for morality succumbing to obedience is the relief of responsibility that occurs when an authority figure provides assurance to the individuals being ordered that they will not be responsible for any unfavorable consequences.

While the results of Milgram's study are indeed disheartening, some comfort can be taken in knowing it was merely an experiment. Unfortunately, this is not the case with two real-life events: the Holocaust and the My Lai Massacre. Concerning the former:

> World War II didn't end on the battlefield - it ended in a courtroom. The Nuremberg Trials bore witness to some of humanity's darkest hours and revealed the full scope of the atrocities of Naziism, culminating in the execution of many top Nazi leaders (2005).

The defense employed by some of the defendants at Nuremberg was, "I was merely following orders."

Concerning the latter, Dr. Peck has written:

> It is an old maxim that soldiers are not supposed to think. Leaders are not elected from within a group but are designated from above and deliberately cloaked in the symbols of authority. Obedience is the number-one military discipline. The dependency of the soldier on his leader is not simply encouraged, it is mandated (1983, p. 224).

During the Vietnam War, on the morning of March 16, 1968, American ground troops from C Company, 1st Battalion, 20th Infantry of the 11th Light Infantry Brigade moved into a small group of hamlets in South Vietnam known collectively as My Lai. What followed is not entirely clear. What is known with certainty is somewhere between 350 and 500 unarmed, noncombatant villagers were shot to death in various ways. Dr. Peck, chairman of the psychiatric committee that investigated My Lai, later wrote:

> In situations such as My Lai, the individual soldier is in an almost impossible situation. On one hand, he may vaguely remember being told in some classroom that he is not required to forsake his conscience and should have the mature independence of judgement - even the duty - to refuse to obey an illegal order. On the other hand, the military organization and its group dynamics do everything to make it just about as painful and difficult and unnatural as possible for the soldier to exercise independence of judgement or practice disobedience (p. 224).

A second explanation for morality succumbing to obedience is *dispersion of responsibility*. Rabbi Dr. Richard Rubenstein's analysis of the Holocaust includes the characterization of this systematic killing of several million people as a multifaceted division of labor. This genocide was facilitated by involving a great number of people in an assembly-line like process that would detach nearly all of the workers from the final product. Only those at the "end of the line" were aware of the final product - a dead human being. Concerning dispersion of responsibility, Rubenstein admonishes:

> The passing of time has made it increasingly evident that a hitherto unbreachable moral and political barrier in the

history of Western civilization was successfully overcome by the Nazis in World War II and that henceforth the systematic bureaucratically administered extermination of millions of citizens or subject peoples will forever be one of the temptations of government (1987, p. 2).

The Free Will of Others

Joseph Fletcher offered *the most loving action* as the guiding principle for moral activity. The existential philosopher and novelist Simone de Beauvoir provided a different guiding principle for moral conduct: *act to maximize the freedom of others.*

She maintained since our values are largely expressed by our behavior toward others, it is through relationships that we disclose who we are. "To will oneself free is also to will others free" expresses her belief that the guiding principle in our relationships should be acting to maximize the freedom of others as well as holding them responsible for their actions (1954, p. 73).

She emphasized since we cannot completely know what the results of our choices will be, we can never be certain an action is right while contemplating it. However, although we cannot know the specific outcome of a choice, we can accurately estimate whether that choice will contribute to our own or another person's freedom. Hence, a corollary to her guiding principle is treating others as we ourselves would desire to be treated (Malikow, 2014, pp. 44-45).

An extreme expression of de Beauvoir's principle is found in the writing of the *antinatalist* David Benatar. (An antinatalist is one who believes it is immoral to procreate.) Benatar's rationale for antinatalism is presented in his controversial book: *Better Never to Have Been: The Harm of Coming into Existence* (2006). He believes the pleasures that await the unborn are far outweighed by the pain in store for them. Moreover, since the unborn have no choice concerning their existence, they have no opportunity to exercise free will in life's most important question: "To be or not to be?" (*Hamlet*, III, 1). Therefore, the decision to bring a human being into existence goes beyond minimizing the freedom of another; it eliminates it altogether.

Benatar has written: "I am under no illusions. My position, no matter how clearly stated, is likely to be misunderstood" (2012, p. 16). Actually, although his position is easily understood, it is nevertheless controversial. The polemic derives from antinatalism's counterintuitiveness to the human instincts for survival and reproduction.

Education and Nurturing

In the fall of 1960 a six-year-old girl named Ruby Bridges entered the William Frantz Elementary School in New Orleans, Louisiana. She was accompanied by United States Marshals, assigned for her safety. She was the first black child to attend this previously all-white school. Ruby's groundbreaking entrance did not go unnoticed. In addition to the protesting crowd threatening and taunting her were an artist and a psychiatrist. The artist was Norman Rockwell and the psychiatrist was Robert

Coles. One of Rockwell's most familiar drawings is that of Ruby Bridges accompanied by her protectors. One of Robert Coles' many books is *The Story of Ruby Bridges* (1995).

Can goodness be taught? The answer to this question is a resounding "yes" according to several academics who have given considerable attention to this question. In addition to Dr. Coles are Samuel Oliner, a sociologist and Holocaust survivor, William Kirk Kilpatrick, a psychologist and author, and Philip Zimbardo, a researcher well-known for his Stanford Prisoners Experiment. Each believes a child can be nurtured into human decency by education and personal encounters. Coles, who has investigated the moral lives of children for over fifty years, has provided a manual for parents and teachers entitled *How to Raise a Moral Child* (1998).

Responsibility

Existentialism is the philosophical movement derived from and emphasizing free will and personal responsibility. Its earliest expression as a distinct school of thought are the nineteenth century writings of Soren Kierkegaard and Friedrich Nietzsche. Prominent twentieth century existential voices are those of Martin Heidegger, Jean-Paul Sartre, and Albert Camus. In his ironic statement, "Man is condemned to be free," Sartre expressed his belief that people fear their own freedom (1957, p. 23). He maintained human beings have free will and with it comes complete responsibility for their actions and subsequent consequences. "Man is condemned to be free" because there is no escape from this responsibility. Sartre further believed for many such responsibility is intimidating.

Nietzsche is well-known for his declaration, "God is dead" (1974, p. 95). Nietzsche recognized without God or some other absolute moral authority over humankind there is moral anarchy. "Nevertheless, he saw something redemptive emerging from this moral chaos: each of us bears responsibility for constructing and living out a self-determined morality" (Malikow, 2014, p. 16). Nietzsche also believed in two fundamental moralities: "There is a master morality and a slave morality" (1966, p. 260). Those with a slave morality submit to a religion or some other moral authority in order to evade responsibility for their behavior. Such people justify their behavior by saying, "I was merely following orders." In contrast, those with a master morality unflinchingly accept responsibility for their conduct because it is guided by the moral code they have constructed for themselves.

IV. Does the End Justify the Means?

For what shall it profit a man, if he shall gain the whole world, and lose his own soul?

- Jesus, Mark 8:36

The end may justify the means as long as there is something that justifies the end.

- Leon Trotsky

Nothing justifies the deaths of innocent people.

- Albert Camus

"The end justifies the means" is a principle associated with Nicolo Machiavelli, author of *The Prince*, published in 1515 and believed to be based on the life of Cesare Borgia, an Italian nobleman and politician whom Machiavelli served as a counselor. Often this principle is misunderstood as positing any action, regardless of its apparent immorality, is justified if it effects the desired outcome. This misunderstanding results from overreaching Machiavelli's intention. He was not addressing ethics in general but referring to any action a ruler might take to stabilize the government, retain power or coerce resistant subjects. Machiavelli was not advocating unbridled individual activity for personal gain or self-gratification.

Given this limited scope, the principle nevertheless remains ambiguous in its application. President Truman's decision to deploy the atomic bomb, referred to in the previous chapter, persists as controversial even though it stabilized the government of the United States. *The end justifies the means* is a teleological ethical concept lacking criteria for determining what constitutes a necessary end. Because of this deficit, it cannot be employed alone for moral decision-making. *Value theory* provides what this principle lacks. Value theory is the subcategory of philosophy that addresses the question: *What are the factors that make one thing worth more than another?* Because it is a significant subdivision of philosophy, this chapter is not the place for a concentrated study of the guidelines it provides. Instead, the following two examples clarify the necessity of value theory for moral decision-making.

The proliferation of Canada geese, described in Chapter II, provided the occasion for an intense debate among the citizens of Winchester, Massachusetts in spite of their agreement on the seriousness of the problem. The debate derived from their disagreement on whether the problem was sufficiently severe to necessitate killing the geese. Implicit in their debate was the question: Which is more important, preservation of annoying wildlife or maintenance of a pristine town? Clearly, this situation was an instance of competing interests, with the best interests of the residents in conflict with those of the geese. How could the cleanliness and pleasantness of the town be weighed against the lives of the geese? Would the *end* - a clean town, justify the *means* - killing the geese?

On January 19, 1987 a man left Massachusetts General Hospital where he was being treated for a tropical parasite he had contracted sixteen years earlier. He drove to Boston Harbor, parked his car, and committed suicide by drowning. This man was the renown Harvard psychology professor Lawrence Kohlberg, whose research on moral development is described in virtually every introductory and developmental psychology textbook published in the last twenty-five years. *Was Dr. Kohlberg's final act morally wrong?* Does it matter that he had suffered both physical pain and depression since 1971 because of his illness? Does it matter that the prognosis was *the worst is yet to come?* Did the *end* - cessation of his pain, justify the *means* - suicide.

"Hard cases make bad law" is a maxim among jurists (Holdsworth, 1926, IX, p. 423). The situations of President Truman, the citizens of Winchester, and Professor Kohlberg qualify as hard cases. In *Why Johnny Can't Tell Right from Wrong*, William Kirk Kilpatrick characterizes the use of hard cases in the form of dilemmas as "how not to teach morality" (1992, p. 78).

> The question to ask about this stimulating approach is this: Do we want to concentrate on quandaries or on everyday life? ... A great deal of a child's moral life - or an adult's for that matter - is not made up of dilemmas at all. Most of our "moral decisions" have to do with temptations to do things we know we shouldn't do or temptations to avoid doing things we know we should do. A temptation to steal money from her mother's purse is a more common problem for the average girl then deciding whether or not to turn in a friend who is shoplifting (pp. 84,85).

Kilpatrick concedes a discussion of the morality of resorting to cannibalism in order to survive or suffocating a crying infant in order to save over a dozen lives will make for an engaging conversation. However, he cautions, "The danger in focusing on problematic dilemmas such as these is that a student may begin to think that all of morality is similarly problematic" (p. 85). Dilemmas obscure the reality that moral decision-making rarely involves a conundrum.

The question in moral decision-making is not: Does the end *ever* justify the means? Unfortunately, there have been situations in which resorting to cannibalism, suffocating an infant or intentionally killing civilians was a necessary evil. Rather, the question is: What are the criteria for determining *when* an end's worthiness justifies any and every means? Regarding this question, there are at least two possible answers: (1) When it is a matter of life and death. (2) When the damage to be inflicted by the means is minuscule compared to the benefit it will provide.

When it is a matter of life and death.

This guideline is consistent with Immanuel Kant's *categorical imperative* that one person should never use another person as a means to an end (Chapter III). This principle denounces slavery, since it makes one person, the slave, a means to the end of financial gain for another person, the slave owner. There is something else to be derived from this principle: if a human life would be saved by an act that is usually considered immoral, then the act would *not* be immoral. An ordinary instance of this is exceeding the speed limit to transport a person with a life-threatening injury to the emergency room. According to Kant's principle, the end (saving a life) trumps the means (breaking the law).

When the damage inflicted by the means is minuscule compared to the benefit it provides.

The example used in the previous section could also be used in this section. The damage inflicted by exceeding the speed limit is minuscule compared to the benefit of saving a life. A mundane life event is telling a lie when the truth would hurt someone for no apparent reason. The following story serves as an illustration.

The pastor always moved to the back of the sanctuary when the congregation was singing the closing hymn. From there he would give the benediction and dismiss his flock. He would then place himself just inside the front door so he could individually greet the congregants as they exited the church. The pastor enjoyed this concluding ritual and his parishioners never seemed to mind the five or so minutes it required.

An elderly widow was one of the last to receive the pastor's wish for a "good Sabbath." She was the kind of woman to be found in every church, regardless of denomination, and deferentially referred to as "Sister." The pastor was unable to cup her frail and withered hand gently in both of his because she was carrying a pie.

Reminiscent of a child presenting a straight-A report card to a parent, Sister could barely contain her excitement as she placed it in his hands. Regaining the breath she had spent transporting the pie, Sister managed, "Pastor, I hope you and your family enjoy this pie." The pastor knew for this woman, baking a pie was a herculean labor. He responded, "Thank you so much. This will be our dessert today. Have a blessed Sabbath, Sister."

That afternoon, after dinner, the pie's tin foil covering was removed. This unveiling released a delightful aroma that was immediately recognized as rhubarb. A slice was cut for each member of the family as the Pastor informed them their dessert was a gift from Sister. As they had been taught, the children waited until everyone at the table had been served before eating. With the coordination of a team of synchronized swimmers, the family placed the first forkful of pie in their mouths. Too refined to spit out the unpalatable morsels, the pastor and his family swallowed their first—and last—taste of Sister's pie.

Stunned silence was followed by parents and children looking each to the other for unspoken confirmation that in a world with millions of pies they had just sampled the most inedible. The phrase, "It goes without saying" was made for a moment like this. There was no need for anyone to comment on the pie's repulsiveness. The pastor's wife broke the silence, "What are you going to tell Sister?"

The question was rhetorical as well as unnecessary. The wastebasket was circulated to receive each uneaten piece of the pie culminating with the half that remained in the pie tin.

That week the pastor spent as much time contemplating the answer to his wife's question as he spent preparing his sermon. What is one to do with the truth when it would hurt someone and serve no good purpose? To tell Sister her pie was delicious would be a lie, but spare her feelings. Then again, it might encourage her to inflict another pie on his family with other pies to follow. He felt the full weight of simultaneous obligations to the truth and the protection of an elderly woman's feelings. He wrestled with the conflicting duties throughout the week, well aware his children would be watching.

The next Sunday morning, the pastor's thoughts alternated between his sermon and the impending encounter with Sister. He had no idea what he was going to say to her when, she asked, "Did you and your family enjoy the pie?"

He needed Solomon's wisdom and identified with the king when he was confronted with two women claiming the same baby. "Perhaps, like Solomon," thought the pastor, "what I need to say will come to me when I need to say it."

The sermon was delivered, closing hymn sung, and benediction given. The congregants, including Sister, formed a queue for the pastoral greeting. Unencumbered by a pie, she extended her hand to the Pastor. Before he could say, "Good Sabbath," She asked the question, "Pastor, did you and your family enjoy the rhubarb pie?" With neither rehearsal nor hesitation he responded, "Let me tell you something Sister, a pie like that doesn't last long around our house!"

Lying is rather ordinary human activity as well as a moral issue of sufficient significance for a Harvard professor to have devoted an entire book to the subject (Bok, 1978). Lying raises the question of whether an intentional misrepresentation of truth is *always* an immoral act. Kant maintained lying is always morally wrong whenever it inhibits or diminishes an individual's exercise of free will. This includes *lies of commission* (saying something that is not true) and *lies of omission* (withholding the truth). Accordingly, he wrote, "Truthfulness in statements ... is the formal duty of an individual, however great may be the disadvantage according to himself or another" (Malikow, 2011, p. 65). In contrast, Friedrich Nietzsche believed the complexities of life are such that life cannot be managed without, at least, an occasional lie. He wrote, "That lying is a necessity of life is itself a part of the problematic character of existence" (p. 65).

In the story of "The Pastor and the Pie" no apparent damage was done by the Pastor's double entendre. Considerable pain would have resulted if the Pastor had unambiguously described the family's reaction to the pie. According to the principle *the end justifies the means when the damage inflicted by the means is minuscule compared to the benefit of the end* the Pastor's misrepresentation was justified.

This is not to say a person's feelings should always be spared at the expense of the truth. In Amy Chua's *Battle Hymn of the Tiger Mother* she recounts refusing a birthday card from her 4-year-old daughter, Lulu.

> Lulu handed me her "surprise," which turned out to be a card. More accurately, it was a piece of paper folded crudely in half, with a big happy face on the front. Inside, "Happy Birthday, Mommy! Love, Lulu" was scrawled in crayon above another happy face. The card couldn't have taken Lulu more than twenty seconds to make.
>
> I gave the card back to Lulu. "I don't want this," I said. "I want a better one - one that you've put some thought and effort into. I have a special box where I keep all my cards from you and Sophia (Lulu's sister), and this one can't go in there."
>
> I grabbed the card again and flipped it over. I pulled out a pen from my purse and scrawled "Happy Birthday Lulu Whoopee!" I added a big sour face. "What if I gave you this for your birthday, Lulu - would you like that?" (2011, p. 103).

Of course, anecdotes like this account for the controversy surrounding Amy Chua's book and widespread criticism of her parenting. She believes, "it's too idealistic to expect children to do the right things on their own. Also, if you force them to do what you want, you don't have to be mad at them" (p. 104). For her, and obviously not for everybody, the end of sparing Lulu's feelings was not sufficient to justify the means of withholding the truth. The truth was that Lulu had produced something well below her best effort. Amy Chua's determination to nurture her children to strive for excellence justified her rejection of a mediocre birthday card.

The determination of when an end is justified by its means is no simple matter. Some of Winchester's citizens argued that an unpolluted town would justify killing the geese and others disagreed. Some, but not everyone, would argue the cessation of Professor Kohlberg's unremitting pain justified his suicide. Many people would agree that an abortion in order to save the life of a pregnant woman provides a benefit that outweighs the termination of an embryo or fetus. However, even among those who would find such abortions justifiable, are those who would oppose other abortions, citing the end is insufficient for justifying the means.

V. How Is a Moral Decision to Be Made When Obligations Are in Conflict?

Two roads diverged in a yellow wood,
And sorry I could not travel both
And be one traveler, long I stood

> \- Robert Frost,
> "The Road Not Taken"

Duties are not performed for duty's sake, but because their neglect would
make the man uncomfortable. A man performs but one duty - the duty of
contenting his spirit, the duty of making himself agreeable to himself.

> \- Mark Twain

The renown (some would say, notorious) psychiatrist Thomas Szasz posited, "The quality of our life depends largely on concordance or discordance between our desires and our duties" (1973, p. 47). Whenever that which we *ought* to do coincides with that which we *desire* to do, life proceeds without conflict. Whenever there is discord between duty and desire, decision-making is not so easily accomplished. And whenever one obligation is in conflict with another obligation, moral decision-making becomes especially problematic.

A well-known situation of conflicting obligations is found in the New Testament narrative in which Jesus is asked if the Jewish people have an obligation to pay taxes to the Roman Empire. The question was intended as a conundrum in order to discredit Jesus by befuddling him. The Jewish people recognized

God as their only king, thereby rejecting Caesar as their ruler. If Jesus advocated nonpayment of taxes, he would have been branded a traitor to Rome. If he encouraged payment of taxes, he would have lost favor in the Jewish community. His answer adequately addressed what seemed to be conflicting obligations:

> But Jesus, knowing their evil intent, said, "You hypocrites, why are you trying to trap me?" Show me the coin used for paying the tax." They brought him a denarius, and he asked them,
> "Whose portrait is this? And whose inscription?"
> "Caesar's," they replied.
> Then he said, "Give to Caesar's what is Caesar's, and to God what is God's" (Matthew 22:18-21).

According to Jesus, the obligations were not in conflict. Since Rome's requirement was monetary, paying taxes to Caesar would take nothing away from God. Since God's requirement is obedience to the Ten Commandments and 603 other *mitzvah* (laws) found in the Hebrew Bible, adherence to God's law would take nothing away from Caesar. In this instance there only seemed to be a conflict.

However, such is not always the case. Sir Thomas More, Chancellor to King Henry VIII, had to choose between loyalty to his King and obedience to his Pope, Clement VII. When the King determined he would divorce Catherine of Aragon and marry Anne Boleyne, Sir Thomas refused to support Henry's decision and agreed with the Pope's refusal to annul the marriage. This led to More's trial and conviction for treason and execution by decapitation in 1535.

Another instance of a church and state conflict, albeit with less dire consequences, is that of Eric Liddell. An almost certain track and field gold medalist for England in the 1924 Olympic Games, Liddell refused to run on the Sabbath, thereby sacrificing the opportunity for the medal. He resisted the urging of his future king, the Prince of Wales, who tried to convince Liddell he had a patriotic obligation to participate. Liddell remained steadfast in his conviction and did not yield to the Prince's urging.

The practice of medicine also provides occasions for conflicting obligations. Chapter II refers to Dr. Jack Kevorkian's administration of a lethal cocktail (combination of medications) to Thomas Youk who was suffering from Lou Gehrig's disease and requested physician-assisted suicide. The procedure was performed in Michigan, where physician-assisted suicide was and remains illegal. As a result, Dr. Kevorkian was convicted of second degree murder and sentenced to ten to fifteen years imprisonment. He served eight years, was paroled in 2007, and died in 2011 at the age of eighty-three.

As a physician, Kevorkian was confronted with oppositional obligations. When he graduated from the University of Michigan Medical School in 1952 he affirmed the Hippocratic Oath which conferred upon him the obligations to alleviate patient suffering and refrain from administering lethal medications to a patient. In the case of Thomas Youk,

Kevorkian opted for euthanasia, convinced it was the only means for alleviating the patient's suffering.

Kevorkian believed there are cases in which the compassionate thing to do is physician-assisted suicide. This would constitute "the most loving act" advocated by Fletcher (Chapter III). Youk had requested this action and provided written and video recorded informed consent, demonstrating the exercise of free will advocated by de Beauvoir (Chapter III). Further, by addressing Youk as a suffering human being in need of pain relief, Kevorkian placed the patient above the law. Hence, it could be argued Kevorkian acted in a manner consistent with Kant's *categorical imperatives of universality, human dignity, and reciprocity* (Chapter III).

A similar situation, referred to in the Introduction, confronted Dr. Max Schur in 1929 when he administered a lethal dose of morphine to a suffering, cancer-riddled patient. The patient was Sigmund Freud, who had asked Schur to promise, "when the time comes, you won't let them torment me unnecessarily" (Gay, 1989, pp. 642-643). Like Kevorkian, Schur placed the alleviation of his patient's pain above the Hippocratic prohibition of lethal medications.

Another striking occurrence of conflicting obligations confronted helicopter pilot Hugh Thompson on perhaps the darkest day of the Vietnam War. Referred to in Chapter III, it was on that day a United States Army company of infantrymen killed between 350 and 500 unarmed, noncombatant villagers, including women, children, and elderly. First, disbelieving what he saw from a low hover over the My Lai hamlet and then appalled by the wanton, indefensible slaughter he was witnessing, Major Thompson decided to act to stop the killing. Assigned to protect soldiers on the ground, he landed his helicopter and ordered his machine gunners to turn their weapons on the American troops if they continued killing the unprotected Vietnamese.

Thompson is hailed as a hero in sociologist Samuel Oliner's book, *Do Unto Others: Extraordinary Acts of Ordinary People*. There it is written, "The courage of this helicopter pilot and his rescue of innocent Vietnamese civilians at My Lai is a particularly compelling example of an unusual kind of military heroism" (2007, p. 117). Thompson weighed and considered his mission to protect soldiers on the ground against his moral obligation to protect defenseless people and acted in favor of the latter.

Obligations: Origin and Prioritizing

Principles are necessary for prioritizing conflicting obligations. Without guidelines, moral decision-making is left to the feelings of the decision makers. However agreeable or compassionate might be the actions of More, Liddell, Kevorkian, Schur, and Thompson, it would be unwise and unjust to approve of a moral action merely because it emanates from the sentiments of the actor. Lieutenant William Calley, who ordered and participated in the killings at My Lai, *felt* he acted rightly that day. At his trial in 1970 he said:

I was ordered to go in there and destroy the enemy. That

was my job that day. That was the mission I was given. I did not sit down and think in terms of men, women, and children. They were all classified as the same, and that's the classification that we dealt with over there, just as the enemy. I felt then and I still do that I acted as I was directed, and I carried out the order that I was given and I do not feel wrong in doing so (2015).

Yet, nearly forty years later, speaking to a Kiwanis Club in Georgia, he issued a public apology for his role in the massacre:

There is not a day that goes by that I do not feel remorse for what happened that day in My Lai. I feel remorse for the Vietnamese who were killed, for their families, for the American soldiers involved and their families. I am very sorry.. If you are asking why I did not stand up to them when I was given the orders, I will have to say that I was a 2nd Lieutenant getting orders from my commander and I followed them—foolishly, I guess (Nix, 2009).

A prerequisite to prioritizing conflicting obligations is establishing the source of the obligations. Without considering the origins of conflicting duties it would be impossible to prioritize them. For Sir Thomas More and Eric Liddell it was a matter of subordinating an earthly obligation to a heavenly responsibility. This principle was declared by the Apostle Peter when he and the other apostles appeared before the Jewish ruling council.

> Having brought in the apostles, they made them
> appear before the Sanhedrin to be questioned by the
> high priest. "We gave you strict orders not to teach in
> this name (Jesus)," he said. "Yet you have filled
> Jerusalem with your teaching and are determined to
> make us guilty of this man's blood."
> Peter and the other apostles replied: "We must obey
> God rather than men!" (Acts 5:27-29).

For Drs. Kevorkian and Schur it was a matter of
preferring the dying wish of a suffering human being over an
oath. For Major Thompson it was a matter of saving lives rather
than following orders that had become irrelevant to his mission.

Shakespeare wrote, "Conscience doth make cowards of
us all" (*Hamlet*, Act III, scene 1). Jean-Paul Sartre wrote, "Man is
condemned to be free; because once thrown into the world, he is
responsible for everything he does" (1957, p. 23). Navy SEAL
Chris Kyle, the most lethal sniper in American military history,
reflected on his duty with these words, "Every person I killed I
strongly believe that they were bad. When I do go face God
there is going to be lots of things I will have to account for, but
killing any of those people is not one of them" (2015).
Prioritizing obligations, conflicting as well as non-conflicting,
requires conscience and a willingness to take responsibility.

Thought Exercise: "The Confession"

Father Gabriel hears the confession of a man whose voice the priest recognizes. He is certain the confessing man is X. The confession is shocking and disturbing. X confesses to having sexually abused his eight-year-old niece, the daughter of his sister.

Father Gabriel appeals to the man to tell his sister what he's done and have her arrange counseling for her daughter. Further, the priest advises X to end all contact with his niece and seek out counseling for himself without disclosing anything specific that would require the counselor to act as a mandated reporter. (As a priest, Father Gabriel is not a mandated reporter and is required to maintain "priest - penitent confidentiality.")

Questions for Consideration

1. In your opinion, does Father Gabriel have a moral obligation beyond the counsel he has given X?

2. Is it justifiable to exempt the clergy from being "mandated reporters" while teachers, physicians, and mental health professionals are not exempt? (Note: Attorneys are not legally required to report suspected or known child abuse, but in some jurisdictions they are permitted to use their discretion.)

3. In a criminal proceeding, a spouse cannot be compelled to testify against a spouse. This would include a case of child abuse.

What is the reason for this feature of the law? In your opinion, is it a necessary and important feature?

VI. Are Feelings Sufficient for Moral Guidance?

Morals excite passions, and produce or prevent actions. Reason itself is utterly impotent in this particular. The rules of morality, therefore, are not conclusions of our reason.
- David Hume

About morals, I only know that what is moral is what you feel good after and what is immoral is what you feel bad after.
- Ernest Hemingway

George's killing of Lenny in John Steinbeck's *Of Mice and Men* (Chapter III) is a literary illustration of passion prevailing over the rules of morality. Ordinarily, shooting an unsuspecting man who has not expressed a desire to die is a nefarious act. However, in this case it is arguably compassionate.

To move from fiction to real-life, in 1984 at the De Soto County courthouse in Hernando, Mississippi, a young attorney named John Grisham witnessed the testimony of a twelve-year-old rape victim. He noted several of the jurors cried as the girl gave her testimony and wondered, "What if the father of this girl killed his daughter's assailants? Would a jury find it in their collective heart to convict the father of murder?" In his spare time Grisham began work on his first novel, *A Time to Kill*, in which he explored what might happen if a father killed the men who raped his daughter. The novel, first published in 1989, became a bestseller.

Are feelings sufficient for moral guidance? In *A Time to Kill* the father, Carl Lee Hailey, felt vengeance justified murdering his daughter's rapists. Subsequently, the jurors empathized with him and found him not guilty by reason of *irresistible impulse*. (At the time of the crime, the defendant lacked the capacity to conform his behavior to a requirement of the law.)

In a book of a different genre, Dr. Atul Gawande describes a case of necrotizing fasciitis, a condition in which a flesh eating bacteria invades the body. The bacteria is highly resistant to medication and the treatment often requires amputation of an affected limb. In *Complications: A Surgeon's Notes on an Imperfect Science*, Gawande's colleague explains the decision to not amputate the leg of a young woman with necrotizing fasciitis. Dr. Thaddeus Studdert, the surgeon in charge of the woman's case, was able to save her leg by laboriously removing the infected tissue (debridement). Reflecting on his decision, Studdert said to Gawande:

> I thought about a BKA (below the knee amputation), even an AKA (above the knee amputation). She was such a young girl. It may seem harsh to say, but if it was a sixty-year-old man I would have taken the leg without question. This was partly, I think, a purely emotional unwillingness to cut off the limb of a pretty twenty-three-year-old - the kind of sentimentalism that can get you in trouble (2002, p. 244).

Granted, this was more a medical than a moral decision.

- emotion drives decisionmaking

Nevertheless, it demonstrates the influence of emotion even in a matter of medical science. Gawande expressed approval and understanding of Studdert's decision: "In the absence of algorithms and evidence about what to do, you learn in medicine to make decisions by feel. You count on experience and judgment. And it is hard not to be troubled by this" (p. 237).

Even in a situation in which there is an algorithm, without the influence of emotion the action taken might be questionable. A lack of feeling in decision-making is integral to the plot of the science fiction movie, "I Robot." Set in the year 2035, Detective Del Spooner (played by Will Smith) strongly dislikes the robots that have been developed to serve human beings by doing their manual labor. The reason for this antipathy is an automobile accident in which Spooner's car was forced off a bridge and into the water below. Another car, with an eleven-year-old girl inside, also was forced off the bridge and, along with Spooner's car, sinking fast. A robot jumped into the water and rescued Spooner, who was protesting, trying to redirect the robot to save the girl. Devoid of emotion, the robot responded: "Your probability of survival is forty-five percent; the child's is eleven percent." The girl drowned.

Of course, affirming moral or any other type of decision-making predominantly on the basis of emotion is a slippery slope. Intense feelings can motivate reprehensible as well as commendable behavior. Adolf Eichmann, who was instrumental in carrying out the Holocaust, said of himself, "I will leap laughing into my grave because the feeling that I have five million human beings on my conscience is for me a source of extraordinary satisfaction" (Knappmann, 1997, p. 335). Obviously he felt he had contributed to something good.

Nevertheless, for some, feelings are sufficient for moral decision-making. Recall Ernest Hemingway's observation introducing this chapter: "About morals, I only know that what is moral is what you feel good after and what is immoral is what you feel bad after" (2015). With all due respect to Hemingway, the indispensable question is whether feelings *alone* are trustworthy for making morally right decisions. The Apostle Paul understood they are not and wrote, "My conscience is clear, but that does not make me innocent. It is the Lord who judges me" (1 Corinthians 4:4). Jiminy Cricket's advice to Pinocchio, "Always let your conscience be your guide," actually is not good counsel. To act solely on the basis of feelings disregards the reality that conscience can be contaminated by self-interest, fear or pride. This is not to say conscience has no value. To ignore conscience and give blind obedience to authority accounts for the atrocity at My Lai (Chapter V).

Moral decision-making involves subjective feelings and objective principles. The celebrated attorney Clarence Darrow recognized this and elaborated that feelings not only precede principles, they determine them. In a debate with anthropologist Frederick Starr, Darrow posited:

Man does not live by rules. If he did, he would not live. He lives by his emotions, his instincts, his feelings; he lives as he goes along. Man does not make rules of life and then live according to those rules; he lives and then makes rules of life (1920).

Writing nearly a century later, social psychologist Jonathan Haidt came to the same conclusion:

> Moral intuitions arise automatically and almost instantly, long before moral reasoning has a chance to get started, and those first intuitions tend to drive our later reasoning. ... Keep your eye on intuitions, and don't take people's moral arguments at face value. They are mostly post hoc constructions made up on the fly, crafted to advance one or more strategic objectives (2012, p. xiv).

If Darrow and Haidt are correct in their shared observation that reason is the servant and intuition the master, then what is the function of reason? Haidt's answer is:

> We do moral reasoning not to reconstruct the actual reasons why *we ourselves* came to a judgment; we reason to find the best possible reasons why *somebody else ought to join us* in our judgment (p. 44).

There is a saying that if you're not a liberal when you're twenty then you have no heart and if you're not a conservative when you're forty then you have no head. Responsible moral decision-making not only *involves* both reason and emotion, it *requires* them. Professor Haidt also has written, "Psychopaths reason but don't feel (and) babies feel but don't reason" (pp. 61,63). When heart and head are not in accord, determining a moral course might be complicated; possibly to the extent that it poses a dilemma. Certainly life would be much easier if morality were less complicated. But it is not. Hence the need for *ethical deliberation* (Introduction).

VII. Is Justice Always Morally Right?

He has showed you, O man, what is good. And what does the Lord require of you? To act justly and to love mercy and to walk humbly with your God.
- Micah 6:8

The law is constantly based on notions of morality.
- Byron R. White, Supreme Court Justice

The law is not the property of lawyers, nor is justice the exclusive province of judges and juries. In the final analysis, true justice is not a matter of courts and law books, but of a commitment in each of us to liberty and mutual respect.
- President Jimmy Carter

On June 2, 2010, Armando Gallaraga, a pitcher for the Detroit Tigers, retired twenty-six consecutive Cleveland Indians. He appeared to have achieved the so-called perfect game in which no batter reaches base when the twenty-seventh Indian batter hit a routine ground ball fielded by the Tigers' first baseman and tossed to Gallaraga covering first base for the final out. The celebration of this rare event turned to protest when first base umpire Jim Joyce made an obvious error and called the runner safe, depriving Gallaraga of what would have been the twenty-third perfect game in major league baseball's 135 year history.

Unlike football, baseball had no provision for a video tape review and reversal of an incorrect call by an umpire. When Joyce saw the replay after the game he admitted his error. The only person with the authority to overrule Joyce's call was the Commissioner of Major League Baseball, Bud Selig. He refused to do so, reasoning it would be the first time a Commissioner overturned an umpire's judgment call and would establish an unwise precedent. Selig's decision was consistent with a principle of jurisprudence: *the law is concerned with neither right nor wrong – only precedent.* Was justice served by the Commissioner's decision? His critics argue that precedent should be set aside when it perpetuates an obvious injustice. Selig's supporters posit that without strict adherence to precedent there is no reliable system for dispensing justice.

Universal and Particular Justice

Aristotle's philosophy of justice, presented in the *Nichomachean Ethics*, makes a distinction between *universal justice –* that which is absolutely morally right, and *particular justice –* that which is right relative to a specific situation. In a perfect society moral absolutes could determine justice in every situation. However, specific situations sometimes require a deviation from moral absolutes if justice is to be served. For instance, truth-telling is a moral absolute and therefore a part of universal justice. Still, as much as honesty is respected as a virtue, there are times when withholding the truth or even lying might serve a greater good. If telling a lie would save a life it would be justifiable as a contribution to particular justice. Returning to the Commissioner's decision, his strict adherence to precedent is an instantiation of *universal justice.* Had he suspended the rule and overturned the umpire's call it would have been an instantiation of *particular justice*.

Justice, one of the Four Cardinal Virtues, is sufficiently complicated to warrant three subcategories: distributive, compensatory, and retributive. The balance of this chapter addresses each of these separately.

Distributive Justice

Distributive justice is concerned with an equitable share of benefits and burdens. *Equal* and *equitable* are not synonyms. The former means "same in amount;" the latter means "proper and fair." Consider four people who receive the bill for the lunch they have enjoyed together. If they decide to pay *equally* they will simply add a tip to the amount and divide by four. If they determine the amount each will contribute according to the cost of each meal and drink, they will be contributing *equitably*.

A *Los Angeles Times* news story provides a remarkable example of a questionable distribution of burden.

"Father 30 Times Over Seeks Break in Child Support"

Desmond Hatchett, 33, is something of a local celebrity in Knoxville, Tenn. In 2009, in a t.v. interview, he proclaimed, "I'm done!" - that he wouldn't father more children.

Now, with 30 children by 11 women, he wants a break on child-support payments. The youngest is a toddler; the oldest is 14.

Hatchett has a minimum wage job, and he struggles to make ends meet. He's required to turn over 50 percent of his wages for chld support – the maximum under law (*The Huffington Post*, 05/18/12).

Hatchett, currently in prison and due for release in 2014, has been incarcerated previously for failure to pay child support. The burden of supporting the children he's fathered has fallen upon their mothers, charity, and public assistance.

A letter to the editor from a Syracuse, New York newspaper addresses the question: "Who decides what makes up a fair share?"

To the editor:

The next time I hear anyone say, The rich should pay their fair share," my hair is going to hurt. Surely, this is a vacuous statement. (Please refrain from saying, "Don't call me Shirley.") Who are "the rich" and how is this determined? What constitutes a "fair share" and who decides?

The Marxist dictum, "From each according to his ability, to each according to his needs" disregards human nature by naively assuming people maximally produce while minimally benefitting. Ayn Rand produced two novels totaling 1,500 pages conveying the philosophy the rich have no philanthropic obligation to the poor. Similarly, Aesop implied that industrious ants are not morally required to subsidize indolent grasshoppers.

Like jurors betwixt dueling experts in a civil case, how are we to determine liability and what it should be? I suggest that before declaring how other people's wealth should be distributed, a bit of self-examination is in order. The Parable of the Good Samaritan (Luke 10:30-37) was told by Jesus in response to the question: "Who is my neighbor?" I submit here we have a starting point for answering the questions, "Who are the rich?" and, "What is their fair share?"

The next time you encounter a panhandler, consider how you are responding and, if you give, how much. Feeling rich? Giving a fair share? These questions are not intended to provoke guilt, but to clarify what you really believe. Then consider this thought from Herman Hesse: "The hardest road is the one that leads a man to himself" (*The Post Standard*, 11/18/11)

Concerning the fair distribution of benefit, there is no shortage of anecdotes describing the sense of entitlement felt by family members and friends of some lottery winners (Stossel, 1998). Requesters often express anger, indignation, or both if they are denied a gift or loan. Bob Harrell, a Texas Lotto winner committed suicide two years after winning $31 million (McVicker, 2000). William Post was on food stamps a year after winning $16.2 million in the Pennsylvania Lottery (Sullivan, 2006). Friends and family insisting on a share of the winnings contributed to the sad ending of both stories.

Compensatory Justice

Political philosopher John Rawls determined, "Procedural justice does not guarantee justice of outcome" (1971, II, p. 14). Ethics philosopher John Boatright has written:

trial by jury ... is not a perfect procedure, but any alternative is worse. So unless we are willing to accept the verdicts of juries – even when the outcome is the conviction of an innocent person or the exoneration of a guilty one – the result is likely to be even more unjust outcomes (1993, p. 94).

Roy Brown is well aware of the criminal justice system's imperfection. In 2009 he received $2.6 million from the State of New York as compensation for fifteen years of wrongful imprisonment for a murder he did not commit. Was he fairly compensated? A similar case is that of Ronald Cotton, sentenced in 1987 in North Carolina to life plus fifty-four years for burglary and rape. After eleven years in prison a DNA test proved his innocence. When he was pardoned by the Governor of North Carolina in 1995, Cotton became eligible for $5,000 compensation from the state.

Jonathan Harr's bestseller, *A Civil Action*, chronicles the lawsuit and settlement of a case of irresponsible waste disposal in Woburn, Massachusetts (1996). Eight cases of leukemia were connected to drinking water contaminated by chemical dumping. The $8 million settlement resulted in $375,000 for each family. How much money is just compensation for a child victimized by cancer?

Is Alex Rodriguez's $250 million salary over ten years fair compensation for playing third base for the New York Yankees? Even "A Rod" might envy rapper and record producer Dr. Dre, who earned $110 million in 2012, the same year singer-songwriter Taylor Swift earned $57 million and country and western superstar Toby Keith took in $55 million (Forbes, 2015). Compare these staggering amounts to the national average salary of a first-year teacher ($35,672) and consider if teachers are adequately compensated (National Education Association website, 2013). (As this book was being prepared for publication, professional boxers Floyd Maywether and Manny Pacquaio earned $180 million and $120 million respectively for their "Fight of the Century.")

Retributive Justice

"Let the punishment fit the crime" is a familiar aphorism to lawyers and laypersons alike. The Eighth Amendment to the *United States Constitution* prohibits "cruel and unusual punishment" for violations of the law. *Retributive justice* is concerned with the question: What constitutes a fair punishment for a given crime?

The opening scene of the movie "The Godfather" is a distraught father meeting with Don Corleone, the Godfather. The man's daughter was savagely beaten by two men who attempted to rape her. She absorbed a horrific beating fending off the rape. The father's anguish was exacerbated when the two assailants received only a suspended sentence for their assault. He asks Don Corleone to have the young men killed. The Godfather refused, saying, "That's not justice; your daughter is alive." He did agree, however, to arrange to have the young woman's beating replicated. The two young men received injury for injury the same beating they administered to man's daughter.

This is *talion* law, characterized by the biblical instruction, "An eye for an eye ..." (Exodus 1:24).

An April, 2013 news story reported the sentencing of a man in Saudi Arabia to medical paralyzation. Ali Al-Khawahir, age 24, was found guilty of stabbing a man in the back, paralyzing him. The court ruled Al-Khawahir must pay his victim approximately $250,000 or Al-Khawahir will have his spinal cord surgically cut to induce paralysis. Ann Harrison of Amnesty International expressed indignation at this instance of eye-for-eye justice: "That such a punishment might be implemented is utterly shocking, even in a context where flogging is frequently imposed as a punishment for some offenses, as happens in Saudi Arabia" (Grenoble, 2013).

Justice: A Thought Experiment

Thought experiments are used in philosophy and other disciplines to investigate the nature of something by constructing a theoretical situation. Often an impossibility in real life, the situation is nevertheless useful for considering and discussing a concept. The following thought experiment concerns justice and is preceded by two actual news events.

First Actual Event

The donor of the first double-hand transplant in Boston last fall has been identified. Forty-year-old Steven Lloyd of New Hampshire died last October after sudden bleeding in his brain. His wife Judi told WCVB-TV she decided to donate many of his organs.

"Even though he and I didn't discuss it, I knew that he would be fine about it because he helped everybody. I made the decision to donate the rest of his organs, why not donate his hands?" The hands went to Richard Mangino of Revere (WCVB-TV, 08/21/2014).

Second Actual Event

In 1978 Lawrence Singleton abducted, raped, and mutilated sixteen-year-old Mary Vincent, severing her arms below the elbows with an ax. Singleton was sentenced to fourteen years in prison and was paroled after serving eight years. In 1997 he was convicted of another murder and sentenced to execution. He died of cancer in 2001 in a Florida prison.

Thought Experiment: Judge Brown's Ruling

In the fall of 2010 Richard McDaniel abducted Brenda Robinson and raped her. Following the rape, McDaniel severed both of Robinson's hands with a hatchet, approximately two inches above her wrists. McDaniel was apprehended and convicted of kidnapping, rape, and acting with depraved indifference to human life. He confessed to all charges after Robinson's positive identification of him in a police suspect lineup.

At trial, the jury did not find in favor of McDaniel's plea of not guilty by reason of mental defect. His attorney, Carlton Graham, argued the repulsiveness of the crime was sufficient to prove McDaniel's insanity. As a previously twice convicted violent felon, McDaniel could have been sentenced to life imprisonment without the possibility of parole. However, prior to sentencing, presiding Judge Mason T. Brown had read a magazine story describing a recent, successful double-hand transplant accomplished at Brigham and Women's Hospital in Boston. (One of over three-hundred such successful procedures in the United States.)

Judge Brown stunned the court when he sentenced McDaniel to amputation of both hands for donation to the United Network for Organ Sharing (UNOS). In exchange for his donation, Brenda Robinson will receive two suitable, matching hands from the organ sharing bank. Acting within his discretion, Brown ruled if Robinson refused the transplant McDaniel still would be sentenced to life imprisonment without the possibility of parole.

A spokesperson for the American Civil Liberties Union, citing its policy against harsh sentences that "stand in the way of a just and equal society" and the Eighth Amendment's prohibition of "cruel and unusual punishment," plan an appeal to have Judge Brown's ruling set aside.

Note: To constitute depraved indifference, the defendant's conduct must be so morally deficient and so lacking in regard for a human life that he or she warrants the same criminal liability as a person who intentionally causes a death. Depraved indifference focuses on the risk created by the defendant's conduct rather than the injuries actually resulting.

VII. Is Justice Always Morally Right?

Questions for Consideration

1. Does Judge Brown's sentence constitute "cruel and unusual" (i.e. inhumane) punishment? If so, why? Do you believe it is likely the ACLU will prevail in its appeal of this sentence? If so, why?

2. Does Judge Brown's sentence go beyond *talion* law (aka "eye-for-eye" justice)?

3. What is your feeling about this sentence? (You are not being asked, "What are your thoughts?")

4. Do you believe this sentence is immoral? If so, why?

5. John Milton wrote of "justice tempered with mercy." Does this sentence violate Milton's principle?

VIII. Can People Be Good Without God?

Why do you call me good? No one is good except God alone.
- Jesus (Luke 18:19)

The assertion that people cannot be good without God is vulnerable to being misunderstood. "It would seem arrogant and ignorant to claim that those who do not share a belief in God do not often live good moral lives" (Craig, 2015). Anyone who would oppose the assertion *people cannot be good without God* by claiming it means all believers are morally superior to all unbelievers would be committing the "straw man fallacy." (The "straw man fallacy" in argumentation occurs whenever an easily refuted position is assigned to an opponent, one the opponent neither stated nor would endorse, and that position is attacked and effortlessly defeated. The refuted position is the so-called "straw man" because it is as easy to knock over as a man made of straw.)

The claim that people cannot be good without God does *not* mean the lives of all believers are morally superior to the lives of all unbelievers. Neither does it mean human beings are incapable of virtuous acts unless they are believers. Moreover, it does not mean believers will always demonstrate moral excellence. History compels the concessions that human decency is possible without God and professed believers have perpetrated evil. Concerning the former, the atheist and existentialist writer Albert Camus was a decent, compassionate man. Regarding the latter, the Reverend Jim Jones orchestrated the mass suicide of nearly an entire congregation, resulting in 913 deaths.

Then what does it mean to say people cannot be good without God? It means that if God does not exist then morality is merely a human convention. Without a moral authority that provides principles of conduct that are binding upon all human beings it is impossible to characterize any behavior as *good* or *bad*. An idea (not a precise quotation) found in Fyodor Dostoevsky's *The Brothers Karamazov* is: if there is no God, everything is permitted. Everything is permitted in the sense that there is no basis for declaring any behavior as bad. The goodness of people is not a question of our ability to perform a commendable act but how *any* act can be considered commendable if there is no standard for praiseworthy actions. This is the question asked by Jesus in his encounter with an unnamed wealthy man, narrated in Luke's gospel:

> A certain ruler asked him, "Good teacher, what must I do to inherit eternal life?"
>
> "Why do you call me good?" Jesus answered. "No one is good - except God alone" (Luke 18:18,19).

The question, "Can people be good without God?" gives rise to a more fundamental question: Is a discussion of *good* even a possibility without a meta-standard for human behavior? Philosopher Richard C. Taylor has written, "Contemporary writers in ethics, who blithely discourse on right and wrong and moral obligations without any reference to religion, are really just weaving intellectual webs from thin air, which amounts to saying they discourse without meaning" (1985, pp. 2-3). Taylor insists moral obligations cannot exist unless there is a being to whom they are owed:

> A duty is something that is owed. ... But something can be owed only to some person or persons. There can be no such thing as duty in isolation. But what if this higher-than-human lawgiver is no longer taken into account? Does the concept of moral obligation ... still make sense? ... the concept of moral obligation (is) unintelligible apart from the idea of God? (pp. 83-84).

Can Definitive Moral Standards Be Derived from Social Conventions or Nature?

If not God, are there alternatives for a moral authority binding upon the human race? The humanist philosopher Paul Kurtz recognized the significance of this question when he wrote, "The central questions about ethical and moral principles concerns (their) ontological foundation. If they are neither derived from God nor anchored in some transcendent ground, are they purely ephemeral?" (1988, p. 65).

Kurtz advocated *secular humanism*, a philosophy that rejects religion as the source for morality and embraces reason and nature for determining ethics. He believed, "The moral principles that govern our behavior are rooted in habit and custom, feeling and fashion" (p. 73). However, yet another concession compelled by history is "habit and custom, feeling and fashion" greatly vary from culture to culture as well as within a culture over time. This is not to posit that all customs are moral expressions. A gentleman rising to stand when a lady enters the room is a matter of etiquette, not morality. The same is true of the erstwhile Japanese practice of a woman walking behind a man, however repugnant that convention might be to some contemporary Americans.

In contrast, the practice of one human being owning another does have moral implications. The anti-Semitic attitude that resulted in millions of deaths in Nazi concentration camps cannot be dismissed as an amoral feeling. Professor Kurtz's observation that social conventions provide moral authority is a reiteration of *moral relativism*, which posits that morality is regionally determined. As such, his position shares relativism's problem of explaining why one culture's attitudes and practices should be preferred over another's.

An unrestrained critic of relativism is the British philosopher Jamie Whyte. He refers to relativism as a "morality fever" and has written:

> Cultural relativism is so absurd that it is hard to believe anyone can be so fevered as to assert it. If it were true, gods, planets, bacteria, and everything else would come into and go out of existence according to what people generally believe to exist. Which they obviously do not... (A) belief cannot be true in Iran but false in Papua, New Guinea. If it is false anywhere it is false everywhere (2003, pp. 154-155).

Another suggested source for definitive moral standards

is nature - the physical world with all its features and living things. Sociobiology, the field of science that attempts to explain social behavior in terms of evolution, theorizes that traits and behaviors that contribute to a specie's survival are genetically transmitted. The problem with this paradigm when it is applied to morality is instinctive behavior is not subject to moral evaluation. John Hick, philosopher and theologian, made the distinction between instinctive and moral behaviors with his hypothetical soldier ant:

> Suppose him to be called upon to immolate himself for the sake of the ant-hill. He feels the powerful pressure of instinct pushing himself towards self-destruction. But he asks himself why he should voluntarily carry out the suicidal programme to which instinct prompts him? Why should he regard the future existence of a million other ants as more important than his own continued existence? ... Since all that he is and has or ever can have is his own present existence, surely insofar as he is free from the domination of the blind force of instinct he will opt for life - his own life (1971, p. 63).

Further, if survival of the fittest is the rule of nature why should human beings have an obligation to any endangered species? No plant, insect, fish or animal is insisting on human assistance in its struggle for survival and reproduction. Moreover, if perpetuation of the human species is the goal from which moral authority is derived, what is special about human beings? Speaking to Rosencrantz, Shakespeare's Hamlet expressed his disdain for the claim that man is the pinnacle of creation:

> What a piece of work is a man! How noble in reason, how infinite in faculty! In form and moving how express and admirable! In action how like an angel, in apprehension how like a god! The beauty of the world. The paragon of animals. And yet, to me, what is this quintessence of dust? Man delights not me. No, nor woman neither, though by your smiling you seem to say so (Act II, Scene 2).

Those who agree with Hamlet might be unimpressed with man owing to his penchant for self-destruction. While evolutionists explain morality in terms of humanity's survival instinct, others point to what seems a determination to bring an end to human existence. Columnist and political commentator Charles Krauthammer has speculated we are alone in the universe in spite of astronomer Frank Drake's probabilistic argument to the contrary:

> Modern satellite data, applied to the Drake Equation, suggest the number (of extraterrestrial civilizations) should be very high. So why the silence? Carl Sagan (among others) thought that the answer is to be found, tragically, in the ... high probability that advanced civilizations destroy themselves.
>
> In other words, this silent universe is not conveying a flattering lesson about our uniqueness but a tragic story

about our destiny. It is telling us that intelligence may be the most cursed faculty in the entire universe - an endowment not just ultimately fatal but, on the scale of cosmic time, nearly instantly so (2013, p. 128).

Conclusion

All the preceding is not intended as an argument for the existence of God or a transcendent being. Rather, the purpose of this presentation is to articulate and evaluate three possible sources for universal moral standards. Christian apologist William Lane Craig believes it is rational to envision moral chaos if a supreme being does not exist:

> If God does not exist, then it is plausible to think that there are no objective moral values, that we have no moral duties, and that there is no moral accountability for how we live and act. The horror of such a morally neutral world is obvious (2015, p. 4).

Indeed, a morally neutral world would be horrific. However, even if it is true that only God could provide a definitive, indisputable code of conduct binding upon humanity, this would be insufficient to *prove* the existence of God. The argument that God must exist lest there be moral chaos is not a compelling argument, however appealing it might be to some. Friedrich Nietzsche believed the *death of God* and its collateral moral chaos was a favorable reality. He believed the absence of a universal lawgiver and judge would force people to construct their own moral codes and take responsibility for living or not living in accordance with them.

The aforementioned problems associated with cultural traditions and sociobiology as sources of moral authority rule them out as possibilities. This leaves a transcendent being as the most rational alternative. Certainly Craig believes this to be the case:

> (If) we hold, as it seems rational to do, that objective moral values and duties do exist, then we have good grounds for believing in the existence of God (p. 4).

In contrast to Craig, physician and author Robert Buckman concluded his book, *Can We Be God Without God?* with these words,

> I am not particularly afraid of dying ... I don't necessarily look forward to it. ... But in my own case, my feelings about my own death and dying are not enough to make me consider a belief in a supernatural God as an option (2002, p. 259).

Epilogue: Chaos in a Parking Lot

The implications of moral chaos can be discerned from the following mundane incident. Smith parks his car in a "Handicap Parking Only" parking place at the supermarket. Jones, not handicapped, correctly noted Smith's car did not have a *handicap parking permit* in the windshield or a *handicap driver* license plate. Further, Jones watched an obviously healthy young man emerge from his car. Smith's female companion said to him, "You're breaking the law. You've parked in a handicap only spot."

Laughing, Smith replied, "Honey, there are no rules in a parking lot."

Upon hearing this, Jones parked his car behind Smith's, which was facing a light post. This pinned Smith's car between the light post and Jones' car.

An hour later Jones, finished with his shopping, returned to his car. An irate Smith confronted him, shrieking, "What the (expletive) is wrong with you, parking like this? Are you crazy or a (expletive) idiot?"

Not the least intimidated, Jones responded, "Honey, there are no rules in a parking lot."

Question: What are your thoughts concerning this incident?

IX. Is a Good Life a Moral Life?

Virtue is its own reward. Doing good for the sake of doing good is true morality, whereas doing good in order to attain happiness is self-serving and mercenary and not truly moral.

- Peter Kreeft

The good life is active, contemplative, somewhat fatalistic, and selfless.

- Daniel Robinson

Epicurus taught, "It is impossible to live the pleasant life without living sensibly, nobly and justly, and it is impossible to live sensibly, nobly and justly without living pleasantly" (2015). What did Epicurus have in mind when he spoke of a pleasant life? It is unlikely he meant a life of pleasure and ease. Many a person has lived a painful, depressed life in spite of having lived "sensibly, nobly and justly." No one lived a more virtuous life than Jesus Christ, yet he was "a man of sorrows, and familiar with suffering" (Isaiah 53:3).

Moreover, the psalmist in the Hebrew Bible was troubled by the pleasant life of the wicked:

... my feet had almost slipped; I had nearly lost my foothold. For I envied the arrogant when I saw the prosperity of the wicked. They have no struggles; their bodies are healthy and strong. They are free from the burdens common to man; they are not plagued by human ills (Psalm 73: 2-5).

The prophet Jeremiah made an equally hyperbolic statement in the form of a question when he asked God:

Why does the way of the wicked prosper? Why do all the
faithless live at ease? You have planted them and they
have taken root; they grow and bear fruit. You are always
on their lips but far from their hearts (Jeremiah 12:1-2).

And Professor Peter Kreeft, when asked if virtue *always*
brings happiness, responded, "It seems that it obviously does
not, for we see that virtuous people are often dour, while the
wicked laugh" (2012, p. 167).

For Epicurus a pleasant life is not necessarily a happy
life. Rather, a pleasant life is a life that is pleasing to the one
living it, and this requires a life that is consistent with that
individual's moral code. Aristotle also believed this and taught a
virtuous life is necessary for *eudaimonia* (overall life contentment).
In his *Nichomachean Ethics* there is this assessment: "He is happy
who lives in accordance with complete virtue and is sufficiently
equipped with external goods, not for some chance period but
throughout a complete life" (2009, 1101a10).

A failure to live consistently with one's own moral code
is exemplified by Reverend Dimmesdale, a character in
Nathaniel Hawthorne's classic novel, *The Scarlet Letter*. Set in
Puritan New England, it is the story of Hester Prynne whose
extramarital affair results in an illegitimate child and the public
scorn that went with adultery. Taking responsibility for her sin,

Hester carries herself with dignity, raising her child and never disclosing the identity of her lover. Her lover, Reverend Dimmesdale, was the community's respected spiritual leader. The minister lives out his years maintaining his image as a man of God. However, his inauthentic life, known only to him and Hester, is described by Hawthorne with these words:

> It is the unspeakable misery of a life so false as his, that it steals the pith and substance out of whatever realities there are around us, and which were meant by Heaven to be the spirit's joy and nutriment. To the untrue man, the whole universe is false – it is impalpable – it shrinks to nothing within his grasp. And he himself, in so far as he shows himself in a false light, becomes a shadow, or, indeed, ceases to exist (1978, p. 107).

In addition, Aristotle believed an upright life is the intended life for human beings. Just as the *telos* (purpose) of a knife is to cut, the purpose of a human being is to live a virtuous life. *The Life We Prize*, a little known but brilliant treatise by the Quaker theologian David Elton Trueblood, includes an arresting observation concerning life and death:

> Each of us is bound to die, and every rational person is highly conscious that his life is short, but there need be no tragedy in this. It is surely not so bad to die, providing one has really lived before he dies. Life need not be long to be good, for indeed it cannot be long. The tragedy is not that all die, but that so many fail to really live (1951, p. 164).

Of course, Trueblood's assertion raises the question: If longevity is not necessary for a good life, then what constitutes a good life? Both classical antiquity and the Christian tradition encourage a life lived in accord with the four cardinal virtues: temperance (self-discipline), fortitude (courage), justice (fairness), and prudence (wisdom). A composite of a good life derived from various philosophical and literary works characterize a good life as one that is lived fully, honorably, meaningfully, existentially, regretlessly, and redemptively. Each of these six characteristics is described in the following subsections.

Live Fully

In his poem, "To the Virgins, to make much of Time," Robert Herrick wrote:

> Gather ye rosebuds while ye may,
>   Old time is still a-flying:
> And this young flower that smiles today
>   Tomorrow will be dying.
> (1648, number 208)

In the movie "Dead Poets Society" Mr. Keating, an English teacher played by Robin Williams, instructs his students that Herrick is imploring the reader to *carpe diem*, translated from Latin to English as, "seize the day" (1989). Edgar Guest expressed the same idea in his poem, "Results and Roses:

> It matters not what goal you seek

IX. Is a Good Life a Moral Life?

Its secret here reposes:
You've got to dig from week to week
To get results or roses.
(1950, p. 23)

Live Honorably

Speaking at the 1992 Boston University Commencement, Fred "Mister" Rogers encouraged the graduates to, "Live in such a way that you'll never be ashamed of the truth about yourself" (05/17/92). Shakespeare wrote of the value of a good name in *Othello*:

> Good name in man and woman, dear my lord, Is the immediate jewel of their souls. Who steals my purse steals trash; 'tis something, nothing; But he that filches from me my good name Robs me of that which not enriches him, And makes me poorer indeed.
> (Act III, Scene 3)

Live Meaningfully

When asked the age-old question, "What is the meaning of life?" Sigmund Freud expressed agreement with Leo Tolstoy when Freud responded, "love and work" (2015). In contrast, Viktor Frankl wrote the meaning of life cannot be reduced to a few words or principles: "In an age in which the Ten Commandments seem to many people to have lost their unconditional validity, man must learn to listen to the ten thousand commandments of which his life consists" (1969, p. x).

He believed the meaning of life changes from situation to situation and in each circumstance it is the individual who bears the responsibility for making that situation personally meaningful.

Live Existentially

Existentialism is a philosophical movement associated with Soren Kierkegaard and Friedrich Nietzsche in the nineteenth century and Martin Heidegger, Jean-Paul Sartre, and Albert Camus in the twentieth century. The hallmarks of existentialism are freedom and responsibility. Sartre wrote, "... man is condemned to be free. Condemned, because he did not create himself, yet, in other respects free; because, once thrown into the world, he is responsible for everything he does (1957, p. 23).

Closely related to living meaningfully, living existentially means individuals are fully responsible for the consequences of their actions. Awareness of this accountability provides moral guidance.

Live Regretlessly

Hockey legend Wayne Gretsky said, "You miss one-hundred percent of the shots you don't take" (2015). And John Greenleaf Whittier wrote, "For of all sad words of mouth or pen. The saddest are these: "It might have been!" (1856, 106-107).

Psychologist Erik Erikson proposed the Psychosocial Theory of Human Development, positing human beings pass through eight stages from cradle to grave. The final developmental task, labeled "integrity vs. despair," is retrospection. It is the stage at which people reflect on their life and accomplishments. If they are content with how they have lived, they face death with a sense of satisfaction which Erikson labeled *integrity*. If, on the other hand, they are disappointed by misappropriated time and unachieved goals they face death with a sense of *despair*.

Live Redemptively

The verb *redeem* means to take that which is unpleasant or distressing and make it useful or, at least, acceptable. *Redemptive* is the adjective form of redeem; redemption is the noun form of redeem. It is not an overstatement to say no one has written about a redemptive life with more clarity and meaning than Viktor Frankl. The epilogue of his classic, Man's Search for Meaning, is entitled "Tragic Optimism." There he enumerates life's three unavoidable tragedies: pain, guilt, and death. Frankl believed everyone has the ability to redeem these inevitable calamities.

Pain can be redeemed by using it to become more compassionate. The poet Betty Sue Flowers captured this idea with these words: "Pain is a mechanism for growth; it carves out the heart and allows room for compassion" (Cronkite, 1995, p. 315). Guilt is redeemable if it leads to repentance and a commitment to change. As for death, Frankl believed life's transitoriness provides "an incentive to take responsible action'" (1959, p. 162).

Ronald Cotton, the wrongfully convicted man referred to in Chapter VII, not only has forgiven the woman who unintentionally, but erroneously identified him, but has co-authored a book with her (2009). In addition, he has spoken at numerous conferences and law schools.

Closing Thought

Peter Kreeft has written, "happiness cannot be separated from virtue," and "the reward for a life of virtue is not external and mercenary but the natural and inevitable consummation of that life itself" (2012, p. 169).

Epilogue: Is Suicide an Immoral Act?

He who does not accept and respect those who want to reject life does not truly accept and respect life itself.

         - Thomas Szasz

Once upon a time there was a man sent by his king to recruit archers for the king's army. The man searched far and wide but could not find even one man sufficiently skilled with a bow-and-arrow to serve the king. Finally, coming upon a small village, the man took delight in what he saw. What he saw were targets painted on the sides of numerous buildings, trees, and hillsides. Especially pleasing to him was that each of the targets had an arrow in the dead center, "bull's eye" location. Excited, he asked the first villager he encountered, "Who is the master archer who lives in this village? He is needed for the king's army."

The man of the village responded, "We have no master archer in this village!"

The king's agent then asked, "But what about all these targets with arrows in the dead center?"

The villager replied with a laugh, "Oh, those! Those are from Shlomo, our village idiot. He goes around shooting arrows all over the place and then paints a target around them wherever they land."

As previously stated, one of the six subcategories of philosophy is ethics - the principles of virtuous conduct. There are two fundamental ethical systems: *teleological* and *deontological.* The former determines moral rectitude according to goals. A teleological approach to ethics is summarized by the well-known maxim: *The end justifies the means.* The latter determines moral uprightness according to standards that pre-exist an action. In the parable of the village idiot, Shlomo is acting in a manner that is *right* from a teleological perspective since the goal is a "bull's eye." However, the irony in the story is that Shlomo establishes a standard that conforms to his prior behavior. From a deontological perspective, his methodology is flawed and his conduct is *wrong.*

Psychology, philosophy, theology, and the law are concerned with human behavior. Psychology investigates *why* people behave as they do. Philosophy, theology, and the law are concerned with how people *ought* to behave. Psychologists make claims from research; philosophers acquire their insight from reflection; theologians claim knowledge from revelation; and jurists evaluate behavior according to conformity to statutes. Suicide can be discussed psychologically, philosophically, theologically, or forensically. In this epilogue the act of suicide is considered as a philosophical topic.

Suicide Considered Teleologically

At the 1987 meeting of the American Association of Suicidologists, Harvard professor and psychiatrist John Maltsberger presented his tripartite explanation of suicide with these words: "Not anger, but rage; not depression, but despair; not loneliness, but aloneness." On May 27, 2006 oncologist

Edward Van Dyke jumped to his death from the fifteenth floor balcony of a Miami hotel *after* having thrown his four and eight year-old sons over the railing to their deaths. The explanation offered for this unspeakable tragedy was Dr. Van Dyke's conflict with his wife. This was rage.

On August 20, 1961, Harvard professor and Nobel Prize recipient, 79-year-old Percy Bridgman, suffering with cancer, shot himself. His suicide note included these words: "It is not decent for Society (sic) to make a man do this to himself. Probably, this will be the last day I will be able to do it myself (Nuland, 1995, p. 152). This was despair.

Judas Iscariot, alienated from the master he betrayed; isolated from the brotherhood of the eleven other disciples; scorned by the Pharisees with whom he had colluded, "went away and hanged himself" (Matthew 27:5). This was aloneness.

The eminent suicidologist Edwin Shneidman, reflecting on over forty years of research on suicide, wrote:

> As I near the end of my career in suicidology, I think I can now say what has been on my mind in as few as five words: *Suicide is caused by psychache.* Psychache refers to the hurt, anguish, soreness, aching psychological *pain* in the psyche, the mind (1993, p. 147).

Psychache is the emotional pain for which there is no opiate; it is responsible for the drama in the mind that drives suicidal thinking. Van Dyke, Bridgman, and Judas all suffered with psychache, each of a different type.

In addition to rage, despair, and aloneness, other expressions of psychache are guilt, humiliation, and meaning-lessness. Judith Guest's bestselling novel, *Ordinary People*, is the story of Conrad Jarrett, a suicidal adolescent who is overcome with guilt having survived the boating accident in which his brother drowned. The Hebrew historical book II Samuel recounts the suicide of King Saul, who fell on his sword to avert his torture and humiliation at the hands of the Philistines. Reminiscent of the book of Ecclesiastes' refrain, Carl Jung diagnosed meaninglessness as the psychiatric-philosophical problem of many of his patients:

> Almost a third of my cases are suffering from no clinical-ly definable neurosis, but from the senselessness and emptiness of their lives. It seems to me ... that this can be described as the general neurosis of our time (1933, p. 61).

Suicide to end the painful states of rage, despair, alone-ness, guilt, humiliation, or meaninglessness is *right* - teleologically speaking. However, teleologically is not the only way to address suicide.

Suicide Considered Deontologically

Immanuel Kant wrote, "Suicide is not an abomination because God has forbidden it; it is forbidden by God because it is abominable" (Evans and Farberow, 1988, p. 179). As previously stated, *deontology* derives from the Greek word for *duty*. Religious prohibitions of suicide are grounded in one's duty to be obedient to the deity or deities. The biblical injunction, "Thou shalt not kill" includes the killing of one's self (Exodus 20:13; Deuteronomy 5:17). Owing to the sacredness of life, the Hindu teaching of *ahimsa* requires nonviolence to all living things. In Islam, suicide is forbidden because it violates *kismet* - one's appointed destiny. The martyred Lutheran pastor, Dietrich Bonhoeffer, reasoned similarly: "God has reserved to Himself the right to determine the end of life, because He alone knows the goal to which it is His will to lead it" (Grollman, 1988, p. 21).

In his *Summa Theologica* St. Thomas Aquinas gave three reasons why suicide is unlawful: it is contrary to the law of nature; it injures the community; and it is usurpation of a divine prerogative.

The philosophical arguments against suicide offered by Socrates and Plato derive from their conviction that human beings are the property of the gods and, therefore, have no right to do away with that which belongs to the gods. Plato wrote:

> I believe that this much is true: that the gods are our keepers and we men are one of their possessions ... So, if you look at it in this way I suppose it is not unreasonable to say that we must not put an end to ourselves until God sends some compulsion (Plato, 1962, p. 105).

The British jurist Sir William Blackstone considered suicide an act of disobedience against the laws of God and man:" ... the suicide is guilty of a double offence, one spiritual, in invading the prerogative of the Almighty, and rushing into His

101

presence uncalled for; the other temporal, against the king, who hath an interest in the preservation of all his subjects" (1765-69, Book IV).

Shakespeare wrote of the poet's ability to convert concepts into concrete realities: "(The poet) gives to airy abstraction a local habitation and a name" (*A Midsummer Night's Dream*, v, i, 16-17). Is *altruistic suicide* an airy abstraction for which there is no corresponding reality in human experience? Kay Redfield-Jamison's memoir, *An Unquiet Mind*, begins with her description of an Air Force pilot who stayed with his malfunctioning plane until it crashed in an isolated wooded area, instead of ejecting and risking that the plane would crash in a schoolyard filled with children (Chapter II). Suicide is not the word that immediately comes to mind when learning of this heroic act. It is only when this pilot's death is held in juxtaposition to the definition of suicide that his death is considered self-inflicted. In so-called altruistic suicides, death is the consequence of a decision to act unselfishly. If there is some further purpose served by a self-determined death then it is counter-intuitive to see it as a suicide. The question of the legitimacy of altruistic suicide as a philosophical or psychological category is an interesting question worthy of a separate essay (Malikow, 2008). The question is raised here to assure the reader that a philosophical treatment of suicide should include the possibility that some suicides are altruistic.

Conclusion

Thomas Szasz has written:

Suicide is a fundamental human right. This does not mean that it is morally desirable. It only means that society does not have the moral right to interfere, by force, with a person's decision to commit this act (Szasz, 1973, p. 67).

Obviously, Dr. Szasz believes an individual's life is the possession of that individual and the person who opts for suicide is not acting immorally. It is also obvious that he is begging the question under consideration. If an individual has an obligation to someone or something other than the herself, then Szasz has not spoken definitively.

"Hard cases make bad law" is a maxim among jurists (Holdsworth, 1926, IX, p. 423). To establish a principle that addresses the morality of suicide from hard cases would be unwise. Those who take that approach would find themselves, eventually, firmly of two minds. The hard cases that follow are intended to underscore the complexity of the issue and the impossibility of reaching an unassailable conclusion.

Suicide is morally wrong when it is a permanent solution to a temporary problem. Dr. Shneidman has written:

Every single instance of suicide is an action by the dictator or emperor of your mind. But in every case of suicide, the person is getting bad advice from a part of the mind, the inner chamber of councilors, who are temporarily in a panicked state and in no position to serve the person's long-range interests (1996, p. 165).

Physician and author Sherwin Nuland made a similar

observation when addressing suicide among the elderly:

> I have more than once seen a suicidal old person emerge from depression and rediscovered thereby a vibrant friend. When such men or women return to a less despondent view of reality, their loneliness seems to them less stark and their pain more bearable because life has become more interesting again and they realize that there are people who need them (1995, p. 152).

The suicidal person who can reframe a seeming hopeless situation into one that is hopeful can move from despair and meaninglessness to a more optimistic view and expectation of better things to come. The philosopher Eric Hoffer aborted his suicide when, after taking poisonous oxalic acid crystals into his mouth, literally looked down the road and had a "sudden vision of life as an endless road" (Hoffer, 1983, p. 24). His deadening routine of "walking, eating, reading, and scribbling" (p. 21) was superseded by:

> ... an alternative I had not thought of ... I must get out on the road which winds from town to town. Each town would be strange and new; each town would proclaim itself the best and bid me take my chance. I would take them all and never repent. I did not commit suicide, but on that Sunday a workingman died and a tramp was born (1983, p. 25).

Quadriplegic artist Randy Souders was challenged to

reframe his life at age seventeen when he injured his spinal cord in a diving accident. "At the early stage (of rehabilitation) ... so many things are closed to you," reflected Souders (Smith and Plimpton, 1993, p. 147). Determined to direct his attention to what he *could* do rather than what he *could not*, he is now a painter with over 1,500 galleries that have carried his work. Reframing can take a person from the despair of the life that is to the possibilities of the life that could be. Suicide is morally wrong when one presumes that his or her future is set when it is not.

Also, suicide is morally wrong when responsibilities to survivors are abandoned. It is no small matter when a parent commits suicide, relegating the surviving spouse to single-parent status and introducing children to suicide as a coping mechanism. John Donne's reflection, "No man is an island, entire of itself" is not a platitude (*Meditation XVII*, 1624).

Equal and opposing arguments can be made for the position that suicide is not morally wrong. The suicide of a mentally ill person is a psychiatric event, not a moral failure. In March of 1995, after closing hours at the National Zoo in Washington, D.C., Margaret Davis King cleared several barriers to the lions' outdoor enclosure. The thirty-six-year-old woman's mutilated body was found the following morning, barely recognizable as a human corpse. Not surprising is that she was a homeless woman with a psychiatric history that included paranoid schizophrenia. To consider her death as an ethical issue would be irrelevant to anything meaningful.

Shneidman has written:

Suicide occurs when the psychache is deemed by that

person to be unbearable. This means that suicide also has to do with different thresholds for enduring psychological pain (1993, p. 147).

Suicide to bring an end to an unendurable existence is less a moral issue than a psychiatric conundrum. Consider these words of Abraham Lincoln, written to his law partner William Herndon:

> I am the most miserable man living. If what I feel were distributed to the whole human family, there would not be one cheerful face on earth. Whether I shall ever be better, I cannot tell; I awfully forebode I shall not. To remain as I am is impossible; I must die or be better, it appears to me (Malikow, 2007, p. 8).

While Lincoln did not take his life, the list of celebrities whose psychache compelled them to suicide is impressive. It is a list that includes two eminent psychologists, Bruno Bettelheim and Lawrence Kohlberg. Ironic is Kohlberg's signature contribution to the study of human behavior is his theory of moral stages of development.

This epilogue is an expression of an attempt to demonstrate the complexity of suicide as an ethical issue. The definition of *dilemma* attributed to Oscar Wilde is: *a dilemma is a situation in which no matter what you choose, you are wrong*. A resolution to take a moral stand on suicide constitutes a dilemma as defined by Oscar Wilde.

Appendix: Morality in Drama and Documentary

Alive: Based on the true story of the 1972 Andes flight disaster, it includes the crash survivors' discussion of whether to resort to cannibalism in order to survive.

A Christmas Carol: The question, "Do we have an obligation to the poor?" is asked and answered in this film adaptation from Charles Dickens' classic novel. Recommended is the 1984 version with George C. Scott portraying Ebenezer Scrooge. Especially provocative is the scene in which Scrooge is visited by his former business partner Jacob Marley.

A Civil Action: A true story of irresponsible industrial waste disposal addresses the issue of fair compensation for victims. Adapted from the Jonathan Harr's legal thriller of the same title.

A Few Good Men: Is it ever morally right to lie? ("The truth? The truth? You can't handle the truth!") When, if ever, should a moral code be abandoned? These are two questions pursued in this film version of Aaron Sorkin's play.

A Time to Kill: Is there ever a time to kill? The father of a rape victim (a ten-year-old girl) murders the two men who abducted, violated, and severely beat his daughter. Could a jury find it in their collective heart to convict this father of murder? This is the film version of John Grisham's bestseller of the same title.

Chariots of Fire: The true story of track-and-field athlete Eric Liddell, who was prepared to sacrifice an Olympic Gold medal to maintain a religious conviction.

Why Can't You Be More Like Me?
An Introduction to Moral Philosophy

Class Action: A thinly veiled movie presentation of 1970's lawsuits involving the Ford Pinto, a subcompact car with a design flaw. The actual case settlement did not establish fault on the part of the manufacturer. Nevertheless, the movie it inspired provides an opportunity to consider compensatory justice.

Courage Under Fire: An honorable soldier disgraces himself in battle. When a person acts out of character, should it be considered an anomaly or a revelation of actual character?

Crimes and Misdemeanors: In this serious production, written and directed by Woody Allen, an affluent physician arranges the murder of his erstwhile mistress, who was threatening to ruin his life - both personal and professional. Does the end justify the means? To what extent can a person recover from a violation of conscience?

Dead Man Walking: The film, based on the true story of Sister Helen Prejean, chronicles her work as a spiritual guide for a man scheduled for execution.

Doubt: Are feelings sufficient for moral decision-making? A nun lacks evidence, but not conviction, that a priest has sexually violated a boy. Meryl Streep and Philip Seymour Hoffman provide magnificent performances.

Flight: An alcoholic airline pilot's integrity is tested when a lie will preserve his reputation and the truth will ruin his career.

Geronimo: An American Legend: This is a relatively unknown movie in spite of its noteworthy cast (Gene Hackman, Robert Duvall, Jason Patric, Wes Studi, and Matt Damon) and their excellent performances. The morality of forcing an Apache tribe off the land that is their heritage and the wisdom of fighting on in a losing cause are questioned.

Hud: An honorable man and his unprincipled son come into conflict over the future of the family's ranch.

I Never Sang for My Father: Robert Anderson's play in which an adult brother and sister disagree on their obligation to care for their widower father.

I, Robot: The implications of moral decision-making by emotionless robots is part of this story, expanded from a collection of short stories written by science fiction genius Isaac Asimov.

Law and Order: (Two Episodes):
"Bodies:" A defense attorney faces an agonizing moral dilemma in which he must choose between maintaining attorney-client privilege or revealing the location of the corpses of his client's victims.
"Darwinian:" When a homeless man is put on trial for murder the legitimacy of his free will and responsibility are called into question.

Listening to Children: A Moral Journey with Robert Coles: A PBS documentary in which the renown child psychiatrist Robert Coles explores the question: How does a child grow up to be a good person?

Margaret: An intense drama in which a teenage girl accepts responsibility for her part in a fatal bus accident. The scene showing the accident vividly illustrates the "law of unintended consequences."

My Lai: A PBS documentary of one of the Vietnam War's darkest days when American soldiers engaged in the mass execution of an estimated 400 unarmed civilians in a Vietnamese village. It includes the heroic action of one soldier, who refused to participate in following an unconscionable order.

Nuremberg: Tyranny on Trial: "The History Channel's" documentary of the trial of the Nazi war criminals for "Crimes Against Humanity." The validity of the defense, "I was merely following orders" and the morality of the death penalty are addressed in this production.

Of Mice and Men: This 1992 film adaptation of John Steinbeck's classic novel features Gary Sinise as George and John Malkovich as Lenny. At the story's end George shoots an unsuspecting Lenny in an act of compassion.

Prohibition: A Ken Burns documentary providing six hours of presentation on the history of Prohibition, including two chapters that address moral issues: "Hatchetation" chronicles the calling of Carrie Nation, a radical force in the temperance movement. "Scofflaws" describes the widespread disregard for Prohibition that eventually brought it to an end.

Seven Pounds: An unusual role for Will Smith is his moving portrayal of a guilt-ridden man who embarks on an altruistic life culminating in his suicide.

The Mission: The story of two priests, Father Gabriel (Jeremy Irons) and Father Rodrigo (Robert DeNiro) who are moved by their consciences to act differently.

The Sunset Limited: A Cormac McCarthy play in which a nihilistic, suicidal college professor (Tommy Lee Jones) and born-again, ex-convict transit worker (Samuel L. Jackson) discuss the meaning of life.

12 Angry Men: Reginald Rose's classic play in which a jury deliberates in a murder trial, dramatizing a disturbing deficiency in the criminal justice system..

Unfaithful: The results of an extramarital affair provide a powerful illustration of the "law of unintended consequences." A well-performed production that also raises the question of personal responsibility.

Glossary

Aesthetics: The subcategory of philosophy addressing the question: What makes something pleasing or displeasing to the senses?

Agape: One of four Greek words for love, it is "unselfish, outgoing affection or tenderness for another without necessarily expecting anything in return" (Hill, 1987, p. 538).

Altruistic Suicide: One of Emile Durkheim's four categories of suicide. In this type of suicide, the deceased chose death for the sake of another person or other persons.

Amorality: Indifference toward the principles of right conduct.

Antinatalism: Associated with David Benatar, it is the idea that procreation is immoral because it brings into existence human beings human beings into a painful existence without their **consent.**

Categorical Imperatives: Immanuel Kant's reference to principles of conduct that are to be followed regardless of circumstances.

Compensatory Justice: The subcategory of justice concerned with fairness in remuneration for services and reparation for injury or loss.

Consequentialism: Closely related to a *teleological* approach to ethics, it evaluates the rightness or wrongness of an action in terms of its results.

Deontological: Derived from the Greek word for duty (*deon*), it is the approach to ethics in which right conduct is determined by rules binding upon all human beings.

Determinism: One side of the *free will - determinism debate*, it is the belief that authentic choice-making is an illusion owing to the law of cause-and-effect.

Epistemology: The subcategory of philosophy addressing the question: How can we be certain of anything we claim as true?

Equal: In the context of *distributive justice*, it is the mathematical calculation used to divide a benefit or burden into identical amounts.

Equitable: In the context of *distributive justice*, it is the determination of a fair division of benefit and burden.

Ethical Deliberation: Contemplation of the rightness or wrongness of an action by considering the relevant facts and accepted principles of the situation and applying them to determine the action that should (or should not) be taken.

Ethical Theory: The evaluation and establishment of principles by which moral problems might be solved.

Ethics: (1) The subcategory of philosophy addressing the question: Are there standards and methodologies for determining morality? (2) A set of rules provided to an individual by an external source.

Existentialism: A philosophical movement derived from and emphasizing free will and personal responsibility.

Fatalistic Suicide: One of Emile Durkheim's four categories of suicide in which the deceased chose death rather than perseverance in a situation the deceased perceived as hopeless.

Free Will: One side of the *free will - determinism debate* among philosophers and psychologists, it is the belief that human beings have the capacity for authentic choice-making.

Hippocratic Oath: The physicians' pledge to uphold certain ethical principles in their practice of medicine.

Human Dignity: One of Immanuel Kant's *categorical imperatives* that evaluates a moral act by asking this question: Would this action have the effect of diminishing the worth of a human being by treating him or her as a means to an end?

Immorality: Behavior that is contrary to a culture's established principles of right conduct.

Irresistible Impulse: Commonly referred to as a "crime of passion," it is one of three qualifying conditions for "not guilty by reason of mental defect."

Law of Cause-and-Effect: The principle that every event owes its occurrence to a prior reality. This principle provides support for the philosophical, psychological position of *determinism*.

Law of Unintended Consequences: The principle that every action contributes to or causes results that are unplanned, but not necessarily unanticipated.

Logic: The subcategory of philosophy addressing the question: How can we be certain that a conclusion is the result of a reliable reasoning process?

M'Naghton Rule: This refers to the test for criminal insanity to determine if an individual who committed a criminal act is to be considered responsible for that act.

Metaphysics: The subcategory of philosophy addressing the question: Is there reality outside of the material realm that cannot be perceived by the senses or subjected to scientific investigation?

Morality: Beliefs about what is right behavior and what is wrong behavior.

Morals (vis-a-vis Ethics): In contrast to ethics (a set of rules provided to an individual by an external source), morals refer to an individual's self-determined principles regarding proper conduct.

Nichomachean Ethics: One of two ethical treatises written by Aristotle. (The other is the *Eudemian Ethics*.) Both works were eventually edited by others. Both begin with a discussion of what constitutes a happy life and proceed to discuss moral excellence (Greek: *arete*). Aristotle was concerned with the character traits that human beings need in order to live the best possible life.

Noumena: Things as they are in themselves in contrast to how an individual perceives them; objective reality, including reality in the nonphysical realm.

Phenomena: Things as they are perceived by an individual; subjective reality, especially in the physical realm.

Philosophy: Derived from the combination of the Greek words for "love" and "wisdom," it is the study of the nature, causes, or principles of reality, knowledge, or values, based on logical reasoning.

Rational Suicide: Similar to Emile Durkheim's *fatalistic suicide*, in this type of suicide the deceased was of sound mind and reasoned that self-inflicted death is a logical, defensible action.

Reciprocity: One of Immanuel Kant's *categorical imperatives* that evaluates a moral act by asking this question: If you were a king who could decree laws by which others would have to live, would you be willing to live under the laws you would decree?

Redeem: A verb meaning to take that which is unpleasant and make it useful or, at least, tolerable. The noun form of redeem is redemption; the adjective form of redeem is redemptive.

Relativism: The ethical philosophical position that moral absolutes do not exist because there is no transcendent being or other authority over all human beings. Therefore, morality is regionally determined and one society cannot judge another society with regard to morality. This was a defense employed by the Nazi war criminals at their post-World War trials at Nuremberg.

Retributive Justice: The subcategory of justice that addresses the issue of fairness in punishment and sentencing.

Secular Humanism: The philosophical worldview that rejects religion as a source for morality and embraces reason and nature for determining ethics.

Sentimentalism: In moral philosophy the belief that right and wrong exist as feelings experienced by individuals rather than concepts.

Situational Ethics: Associated with Joseph Fletcher, it is a relativistic approach to ethics positing right and wrong do not exist as objective realities. Instead, right and wrong vary according to the circumstances in which an action is being considered.

Sociobiology: The field of science that attempts to explain social behavior in terms of evolution, theorizing the traits and behaviors that contribute to a species' survival are genetically transmitted.

Teleological: Derived from the Greek word for "end" or "purpose" (*telos*), it is the approach to ethics that evaluates an action as right or wrong according to whether it contributes to a desired goal. Colloquially, it is expressed by the aphorism: "The end justifies the means."

Thought Experiment: Theoretical and often impossible situations used in philosophy and other disciplines to discuss a concept.

Tragic Optimism: The epilogue in Viktor Frankl's classic *Man's Search for Meaning* in which he posits life's three unavoidable tragedies (pain, guilt, and death) can be redeemed, and thereby enrich one's life.

Unconscionable: An adjective describing an act or person not restrained by conscience.

Universalization: One of Immanuel Kant's *categorical imperatives* that evaluates a moral act by asking this question: Would the world be a better place if everyone in the world would act as you are about to act?

Utilitarianism: The ethical theory that posits morally right actions are those that result in the greatest good for the most number of involved people.

Value Theory: The subcategory of philosophy addressing the question: What are the factors that give one thing more worth than another?

References

Preface

King, R. (2014). Recovered from Thinkexist.com website September, 2014.

Shaw, G.B. (2014). Recovered from Thinkexist.com website September, 2014.

Introduction

American heritage dictionary of the English language. (1973). Boston, MA: Houghton Mifflin Company.

Johnson, L.T. (2007). *Practical philosophy: The Greco-Roman moralists.* Chantilly, VA: The Teaching Company.

James, W. (1995). "The current dilemma of philosophy." *Pragmatism.* Mineola, NY: Dover Publications.

King, M.L. (1989). *Ethics in America: Source reader.* Newton, L.H., editor. Englewood Cliffs, NJ: Prentice Hall.

Malikow, M. (2013). *The human predicament: Towards an understanding of the human condition.* Chipley, FL: Theocentric Publishing Group.

_____. (2014). *Mere existentialism: A primer.* Chipley, FL: Theocentric Publishing Group.

Matousak, M. (2011). *Ethical wisdom: What makes us good?* New York: Doubleday.

Truman, H.S. (2014). Recovered from Thinkexist.com website October, 2014.

Chapter I

Brennan, W. (1972). Furman v. Georgia, 408 U.S. 238.

Darrow, C. (1924). Nathan Leopold and Richard Loeb Trial. August 22, 1924.

Hatch, O. (2014). Recovered from Thinkexist.com website September, 2014.

Peck, M.S. (1983). People of the lie: *The hope for healing human evil.* New York: Simon and Schuster.

Regan, R. (1968). Republican National Convention speech given on August 31, 1968.

Rubenstein, R. (1975). *The cunning of history: The holocaust and the American future.* New York: HarperCollins.

Chapter II

Aristotle. (2014). Recovered from Thinkexist.com website October, 2014.

Durkheim, E. (1897). *Le suicide: etudie de sociologie.* Paris, France: Alcan.

Grisham, J. (1989). *A time to kill.* Chatham, NJ: Wynwood Press Publishing.

References

Hare, R. (1999). *Without conscience: The disturbing world of the psychopaths among us.* New York: Guilford Press.

Holmbach, P. (1770). "The illusion of free will. Reason and responsibility." *Readings in some basic problems in philosophy.* Belmont, CA: Wadsworth/Thompson Learning.

Jamison, K.R. (1995). *An unquiet mind.* New York: Random House.

Joiner, T. (2011). *Myths about suicide.* Cambridge, MA: Harvard University Press.

Katen, T. (1973). *Doing philosophy.* Englewood Cliffs, NJ: Prentice-Hall.

Malikow, M. (2009). *Philosophy 101: A primer for the apathetic or struggling student.* Lanham, MD: University Press of America.

_____. (2013). *The human predicament: Towards an understanding of the human condition.* Chipley, FL: Theocentric Publishing Group.

Menand, L. (2014). "The Prisoner of Stress." *The New Yorker.* 01/27/2014.

Negri, P. (1999). *The wit and wisdom of Mark Twain.* Mineola, NY: Dover Publications.

Nuland, S. (1993). *How we die. Reflections on life's final chapter.* New York: Random House.

Sapolsky, R. (1994). *Why zebras don't get ulcers.* New York: Henry Holt.

Tennyson, A. (1854). "The charge of the light brigade."

Recovered from The Poetry Foundation website. Harriet Monroe Poetry Institute. Chicago, IL. October 2014.

Wallace, D.F. (2007). *Consider the lobster and other essays*. New York: Little, Brown and Company.

Chapter III

Benatar, D. (2012). *Better never to have been: The harm of coming into existence*. Oxford, UK: Oxford University Press.

Bentham, J. (2014). Recovered from Thinkexist.com website November 2014

Coles, J. (1995). *The story of Ruby Bridges*. New York: Scholastic Paperbacks

_____. (1998). *The moral intelligence of children: How to raise a moral child*. New York: Penguin Group.

Fletcher, J. (1966). *Situational ethics: The new morality*. Santa Ana, CA: Westminster Press.

_____. (2014). Recovered from Thinkexist.com website November 2014.

Haidt, J. (2006). *The happiness hypothesis: Finding modern truth in ancient wisdom*. New York: Perseus Books.

Hill, G. (1987). *The discovery Bible: New American standard version*. Chicago. IL: Moody Press.

Hume, D. (1740). *A treatise of human nature*. Reprinted in 2012. Charleston, SC: CreateSpace Independent Publishing Platform.

References

"Justice at Nuremberg: Tyranny on trial." (2005). "The History Channel." A & E Television Networks.

Kant, I. (2014). Recovered from Thinkexist.com website November 2014.

_____. (1785). *Grounding for the metaphysics of morals: On a supposed right to lie because of philanthropic concerns.* J.W. Ellington, translator. 1993. Indianapolis, IN: Hackett Classics.

Malikow, M. (2014). *Mere existentialism: A primer.* Chipley, FL: Theocentric Publishing.

Milgram, S. (1974). *Obedience to authority: An experimental view.* New York: HarperCollins.

Mill, J.S. (2014). Recovered from Thinkexist.com website November 2014.

Nietzsche, F. (1974). *The gay science.* Walter Kaufmann, translator. New York: Random House.

_____. (1966). *Beyond good and evil.* Walter Kaufmann, translator. New York: Vintage Books.

Pascal, B. (2014). Recovered from Thinkexist.com website November 2014.

Peck M.S. (1983). *People of the lie: The hope for healing human evil.* New York: Simon and Schuster.

Rubenstein, R. (1975). *The cunning of history: The holocaust and the American future.* New York: HarperCollins.

Sartre, J.P. (1957). *Existentialism and human emotions.* New York: Citadel Press. Kensington Publishing Corporation.

Truman, H.S. (1945). Statement by the President of the United States on August 6, 1945. Harry S. Truman Library. Independence, MO.

Chapter IV

Bok, S. (1978). *Lying: Moral choice in public and private life.* New York: Random House.

Chua, A. (2011). *Battle hymn of the tiger mother.* New York: Penguin Group.

Holdswarth, W.S. (1926). *History of English law.* London: Methuen.

Kilpatrick, W.K. (1992). *Why Johnny can't tell right from wrong and what we can do about it.* New York: Touchstone Books.

Malikow, M. (2011). "The necessity of lying." *Philosophy reader: Essays and articles for thought and discussion.* Charleston, SC: Create Space Independent Publishing Platform.

Chapter V

Calley, W. (2015). "The trial of William Calley." Recovered from Wikipedia, January 2015.

Gay, P. (1989). *Freud: A life for our times.* New York: W.W. Norton Company.

Kyle, C. (2015). Recovered from Brainy Quote website on April 27, 2015.

Nix, D. (2009). "Long silent Calley speaks." Columbus, GA: Ledger Enquirer. August 21, 2009.

Oliner, S. (2003). *Do unto others: Extraordinary acts of ordinary people.* Boulder, CO: Westview Press.

Sartre, J.P. (1957). *Existentialism and human emotions.* New York: Citadel Press. Kensington Publishing Corporation.

Szasz, T. (1973). *The second sin.* New York: Doubleday.

Chapter VI

Darrow, C. (1920). "Is the human race getting anywhere?" Chicago, IL: Maclaskey and Maclaskey   (reporters).

Gawande, A. (2002). *Complications: A surgeon's notes on an imperfect science.* New York: Picador.

Grisham, J. (1989*). A time to kill.* Chatham, NJ: Wynwood Press Publishing.

Haidt, J. (2012). *The righteous mind: Why good people are divided by politics and religion.* New York: Pantheon Books.

"I Robot" (2004). Beverly Hills, CA: Twentieth Century Fox Home Entertainment, Inc.

Knappman, E.W. (1997). *Great world trials.* Detroit, MI: Gale Research.

Chapter VII

Cotton, R., Thompson-Canino, J., and Torneo, E. (2009). *Picking Cotton: Our memoir of injustice.* New York: St. Martin's Griffin.

Forbes: Recovered from www.forbes.com on April 24, 2015.

Grenoble, R. (2013). "Ali Al-Khawajir, Saudi man sentenced to be paralyzed in 'eye for eye' justice." *The Huffington Post.* April 4, 2013.

Harr, J. (1996). *A civil action.* New York: Vintage Press. Random House.

McVicker. (2000)."Billie Bob's misfortune." *The Houston Press.* February 10, 2000.

National Education Association website. Recovered on June 15, 2013.

Rawls, J. (1971). *A theory of justice.* Cambridge, MA: Harvard University Press.

Stossel, J. (1998). "The mystery of happiness: Who has it and how to get it." ABC News Special. Airing date: January 22, 1998.

Sullivan, P. "William 'Bud' Post III: Unhappy lottery winner. *The Washington Post.* January 20, 2013.

The Huffington Post (2012). "Father thirty times over seeks break in child support." Reported in *The Los Angeles Times* on May 18, 2012.

The Post Standard (2012). "Who decides what makes up a fair share?" Malikow, M. November 18, 2011.

WCVB-TV. 10/30/2012.

Chapter VIII

Buckman, R. (2002). *Can we be good without God? Biology, behavior, and the need to believe.* Amherst, NY: Prometheus Books.

Craig, W.L. (2015). "Can we be good without God?" Recovered from Reasonable Faith website on 03/18/2015.

Hick, J. (1971). *Arguments for the existence of God.* New York: Herder and Herder.

Krauthammer, C. (2013). *Things that matter: Three decades of passions, pastimes, and politics.* New York: Crown Forum.

Kurtz, P. (1988). *Forbidden fruit.* Buffalo, NY: Prometheus Books.

Taylor, R.C. (1984). *Ethics, faith, and reason.* Englewood Cliffs, NJ: Prentice-Hall.

Whyte, J. (2004). *Crimes against logic: Exposing the bogus arguments of politicians, priests, journalists, and other serial offenders.* New York: McGraw - Hill.

Chapter IX

Aristotle. (2009) *Nichomachean ethics.* Lesley Brown (editor). David Rose (translator). Oxford, UK: Oxford University Press.

Cronkite, C. (1995). *On the edge of darkness: Conversations about conquering depression.* New York: Doubleday.

"Dead Poets Society." (1989). Burbank, CA: Touchstone Pictures.

Epicurus. (2015). "Letter to Menoeceus." Recovered from www.epicurus.net website April 2015.

Frankl, V. (1969). *The will to meaning: Foundations and applications of logotherapy.* New York: Penguin Group.

_____. (1959). *Man's search for meaning.* New York: Washington Square.

Freud, S. (2015). Recovered from Thinkexist.com website March, 2015.

Gretsky, W. (2015). Recovered from Thinkexist.com website March 2015.

Guest, E. (1950). "Results and roses." Recovered from All Poetry.com website April 2015.

Hawthorne, N. (1978). *The scarlet letter.* New York: W.W. Norton.

Herrick, R. (1648). "To the virgins to make much of time." Recovered from All Poetry.com website April 2015.

Kreeft. (2012). *Summa philosophica.* South Bend, IN: St. Augustine's Press.

Sartre, J.P. (1957). *Existentialism and human emotions.* New York: Kensington Publishing Group.

Trueblood. D.E. (1951). *The life we prize.* New York: Harper and Brothers.

Whittier, J.G. (1856). "Maude Miller." Recovered from www.poetry.com April 2015.

Epilogue

References

Blackstone. W. 1765-69. *Commentaries on the laws of England.* Book IV.

Camus, A. *The myth of Sisyphus.* translated: J. O'Brien. 1942. New York: Penguin Books.

Donne, J. 1624. *Meditation XVII.* Recovered from The encyclopedia of suicide. Glen Evans and Norman Farberow (editors). New York: Facts on File.

Evans, G. and Farberow, N. 1988. *The encyclopedia of suicide.* New York: Facts on File.

Grollman, E. 1988. *Suicide: Prevention, intervention, postvention.* Boston: Beacon Press.

Hoffer, E. 1983. *Truth imagined.* New York: Harper and Row.

Holdsworth, W.S. 1926. *History of English law.* London: Methuen.

Jung, C.J. 1933. *Modern man in search of a soul.* New York: Harvest Books.

Malikow, M. 2008. "Altruistic Suicides." *Suicidal thoughts: essays on self-determined death.* Lanham, MD: Rowman and Littlefield Publishing Group.

_____. 2007. *Profiles in character: Twenty-six stories that will instruct and inspire teenagers.* Lanham, MD: Rowman and Littlefield Publishing Group.

Maltsberger, J. (1987). Annual Conference of the American Association of Suicidologists. Sponsor: Harvard School of Medicine. Boston, MA: Copley Plaza Hotel.

Nuland, S. 1995. *How we die.* New York: Random House.

Plato. *Phaedo.* translated: Tredennick, H. New York: Penguin Books. 1962.

Shakespeare, W. 1590 (estimate). *A midsummer night's dream.* v, I, 16-17.

Shneidman, E. "Suicide as psychache." <u>Journal of Nervous and Mental Disease</u>.Vol. 181. No. 3. March, 1993.

_____. 1996. *The suicidal mind.* New York: Oxford University Press.

Smith Kennedy, J. and Plimpton, G. 1993. *Chronicles of courage: Very special artists.* New York: Random House.

Szasz, T. 1973. *The second sin.* New York: Doubleday.

About the Author

Max Malikow is on the faculty of the Renee Crown Honors Program of Syracuse University and an Adjunct Assistant Professor of Philosophy at LeMoyne College. He earned his M.A. from Gordon-Conwell Theological Seminary and Th.D. from Boston University.

His other books include:

Being Human: Philosophical Reflections on Psychological Issues

Philosophy 101: A Primer for the Apathetic or Struggling Student

Philosophy Reader: Essays and Articles for Thought and Discussion

Profiles in Character

Suicidal Thoughts: Essays on Self-Determined Death

The Human Predicament: Towards an Understanding of the Human Condition

Mere Existentialism: A Primer

He is a practicing psychotherapist in Syracuse, New York.